CLIENT INTERVIEW, ATTENDANCE NOTE AND LEGAL ANALYSIS FOR SQE2

Ian Bowden, Stephanie Brown,
and Mohammad Sabuj

Routledge
Taylor & Francis Group
LONDON AND NEW YORK

Designed cover image: Azzurri / Getty Images ®

First published 2025
by Routledge
4 Park Square, Milton Park, Abingdon, Oxon OX14 4RN

and by Routledge
605 Third Avenue, New York, NY 10158

Routledge is an imprint of the Taylor & Francis Group, an informa business

British Library Cataloguing-in-Publication Data
A catalogue record for this book is available from the British Library

Library of Congress Cataloging-in-Publication Data
Names: Bowden, Ian, author. | Brown, Stephanie (Lawyer), author. | Sabuj, Mohammad Z., author.
Title: Client interview, attendance note, and legal analysis for SQE2 / Ian Bowden, Stephanie Brown, and Mohammad Sabuj.
Description: Abingdon, Oxon [UK] ; New York, NY : Routledge, 2025. | Series: Legal practice sqe2 | Includes bibliographical references and index.
Identifiers: LCCN 2024062115 | ISBN 9781032856315 (hardback) | ISBN 9781032856285 (paperback) | ISBN 9781003519096 (ebook)
Subjects: LCSH: Solicitors Qualifying Examination. | Bar examinations—England. | Dispute resolution (Law)—England—Examinations, questions, etc. | Interviewing in law practice—England. | Attorney and client—England.
Classification: LCC KD476 .B69 2025 | DDC 340.076—dc23/eng/20250113
LC record available at https://lccn.loc.gov/2024062115

ISBN: 978-1-032-85631-5 (hbk)
ISBN: 978-1-032-85628-5 (pbk)
ISBN: 978-1-003-51909-6 (ebk)

DOI: 10.4324/9781003519096

Typeset in The Sans
by Apex CoVantage, LLC

'To Bunty and all the girls, with love'
– Ian

'To Gerry and Patty B, with infinite love and gratitude'
– Stephanie

Our thanks to each and every person who helped to choose the front cover of this book, with special thanks to Lucy Yates, Sophia Leonard and Isabelle Boden.

CLIENT INTERVIEW, ATTENDANCE NOTE AND LEGAL ANALYSIS FOR SQE2

Client Interview, Attendance Note and Legal Analysis for SQE2 is the latest title in a new series of books aimed at those preparing for SQE2, providing a comprehensive overview of everything you need to successfully pass the SQE2 advocacy assessment.

This book explains the key principles of oral communication, interview technique, and legal analysis in a clear, concise, and easy-to-understand style. The use of practical examples, from the practice areas set out by the SRA assessment specification, allows such key principles to be effectively introduced and illustrated. The book demonstrates the importance of the three key tenets of listening, questioning, and advising, with a view to ensuring that a matter can be analysed effectively, and effective and appropriate decisions can be made. The book provides a clear and structured approach, with opportunities to apply the relevant principles to the law. Chapters include summaries, key practice cases, practice tips, and exercises to reinforce learning and understanding.

Written by an author team with extensive experience in teaching and practice, this unique book will be essential reading for any candidate wishing to be fully prepared for their SQE2 assessment.

Ian Bowden is a practising solicitor advocate and the LLM SQE Programme Manager at Liverpool John Moores University. He is the author of *Essential Constitutional and Administrative Law for SQE1* and *Essential Legal System and Legal Services for SQE1*.

Stephanie Brown is a solicitor with many years of experience in legal practice and is a legal trainer in a leading Manchester law firm.

Mohammad Sabuj is Barrister-at-Law (Lincoln's Inn) and Senior Lecturer in Law, University of Greenwich.

Legal Practice for SQE2

Series Editor: Rita D'Alton-Harrison

For more information about this series, please visit: https://www.routledge.com/Legal-Practice-for-SQE2/book-series/SQE2

Recognising that competencies are developed over time and increase with experience, this SQE2 series helps to 'grow' the legal professional using guided exercises, self-reflection and elements of independent study. Each textbook in this series is designed to help the reader to master the six legal skills assessed in the SQE2 in the context of specific fields of practice whilst also preparing them for entering a new life in practice. In this way it is hoped that the textbooks will serve as both a workbook and a reference manual to help the reader to build upon and improve their skills at the early stages of their legal career. Each book in the series contains commentary explaining why and how the legal skills are relevant to practice as well as signposting when the inclusion of additional information would increase the quality and effectiveness of the legal professional's work and when the inclusion of certain irrelevant or incorrect information would not. In addition to the six SQE legal skills, the exercises in each book are designed to help with the development of additional skills such as observation, decision-taking, judgment, drafting and retention of information as well as taking the reader through the essentials of procedural rules and practice tasks.

Advocacy for SQE2: A Guide to Legal Practice
Rita D'Alton-Harrison

Client Interview, Attendance Note and Legal Analysis for SQE2
Ian Bowden, Stephanie Brown and Mohammad Sabuj

Contents

Table of cases

Table of statutes

Introduction

Whilst writing this guide to legal interviews and the associated skill of legal analysis, the authors have sought to provide the reader with a guide that demonstrates the link between the academic knowledge, that has been the foundation of legal training programmes for many years, and the reality of completing those processes within a practice setting.

This approach has been taken to ensure that students are able to not only consider the requirements of passing the Solicitors Qualifying Examinations (SQE) but also to ensure that they are confident, effective, and resilient legal practitioners.

Whilst the title is envisaged as a resource that can be used beyond considerations of the SQE2 Practical Skills Assessments, it should be noted that content that is directly related to SQE-assessed skills is signposted. In addition, we use exercises, problem-based scenarios, and case studies to ensure that the reader is developing their own practice in this vital area.

The vital role of interviewing within the client journey is recognised within the professional conduct rules, that underpin both professional practice and the guidance provided within this text.

1 Oral Communication Skills

An Introduction

Key Chapter Points

1. This initial chapter sets the scene for how vital oral communication skills are for those who work within legal practice.
2. On an average day, a Solicitor will speak with clients, courts, representatives for other parties, colleagues, and other business professionals. Each of these 'audiences' requires a wide range of skills of professionalism, empathy, tone, consideration of context, and language.
3. Professional rules and codes of conduct are a constant within the role of the legal professional in the completion of interviewing and advice processes.
4. A competent legal professional carries out their role to the expected standards as set out by professional bodies and associated codes.
5. An ethical legal professional is expected to be honest, have integrity, and adhere to regulations and standards to maintain public trust and confidence in the profession.
6. There are many facets to the process of legal interviewing, with no one correct approach.
7. The SQE requirements in this area require candidates to combine knowledge, skills, ability, and professional values to achieve a successful outcome.

1.1 Statement of Solicitor Competence

To ensure that students can understand how interviewing and legal analysis are incorporated into the route to qualified status, it is important to first consider professional competence.

The SRA's competence statement identifies the skills, knowledge, and behaviours expected of solicitors and those who seek to join the roll. It is in three parts:

- The Statement of Solicitor Competence defines the standards that a solicitor must adhere to for them to perform their role effectively. The statement is designed to ensure that there is an identified standard that applies to both the service provider (the legal professional) and the service user (the customer). It is this standard that SQE students are required to demonstrate.

DOI: 10.4324/9781003519096-1

- Threshold standard. Whilst the Statement of Solicitor Competence outlines a general standard of performance, the Threshold Standard provides a more detailed framework. Although there are five levels of competency, the Solicitors Regulation Authority (SRA) designates level 3 as the standard required at the point of qualification. Level 3 states as follows:
  - Functioning knowledge
    Identifies the legal principles relevant to the area of practice and applies them appropriately and effectively to individual cases.
  - Standard of work
    Acceptable standard achieved routinely for straightforward tasks. Complex tasks may lack refinement.
  - Autonomy
    Achieves most tasks and is able to progress legal matters using own judgment, recognising when support is needed.
  - Complexity
    Able to deal with straightforward transactions, including occasional, unfamiliar tasks which present a range of problems and choices.
  - Perception of context
    Understands the significance of individual actions in the context of the objectives of the transaction/strategy for the case.
  - Innovation and originality
    Uses experience to check information provided and to form judgments about possible courses of action and ways forward.
- The Statement of Legal Knowledge outlines the knowledge that solicitors are required to demonstrate at the point of qualification. The legal knowledge component is aligned directly with the Assessment Specification for SQE1. Regarding the SQE assessments, it should be noted that the key areas under consideration are:
  - Property Practice
  - Wills and the Administration of Estates
  - Professionalism and Ethics

1.2 The Importance of Oral Communication to the Legal Professional

When considering the everyday role of the legal professional, it is easy to imagine a wide range of interactions with individuals and organisations across a range of contexts. From arriving at the office in the morning and greeting colleagues through to the first telephone call with a client, responding to e-mails from representatives for other parties, and speaking with the court regarding an ongoing matter.

At the very heart of the role is the ability to communicate with verbal communication, a vital skill in everything from taking instructions, updating clients, liaising with counsel, and negotiating settlements.

Even the SRA underscores the importance of communication. Contained within their consumer guidance documentation, it is stated that:

> Effective communication from the very beginning is essential to make sure everything goes smoothly, and you don't get any nasty surprises later on. You can communicate with your solicitor in person, by telephone, by email, or any combination of these. It is important that you establish from the start what means of communication you will ordinarily use. This may happen during an initial interview.[1]

With this expectation so clearly central to the client/solicitor relationship, it is of vital importance to get this right if we are to avoid dissatisfied clients, negative reviews, and even the possibility of formal complaints.

Whilst it is true to say that legal professionals are often more comfortable with traditional forms of written communication, it is important for the modern lawyer to be well-versed in a whole manner of contact systems. These include letters and e-mails, but increasingly require ability in the use of Teams, Zoom, Client-Specific portals, WhatsApp, and face-to-face meetings.

1.3 Combining Oral and Written Communication Skills

It is often the case that legal professionals will be heard to say the line, 'I will confirm that in writing', and this is very true of many stages that encompass roles within practice. One of the key stages where this is the case is at the outset of the legal matter. At this stage, the instructions given by the client will often be confirmed in writing to ensure that the details are correct and that the legal professional has an evidential trail that confirms at each stage what was said and what was asked for.

This same point is reiterated at many stages in the claims process, from the provision of paperwork to a client for them to check and append with a statement of truth even to witness evidence before a court. This may, on the surface, seem to be the ultimate in oral communication within the legal process. However, it is a well-established process that statements are simply submitted in writing with only cross-examination forming a strictly verbal aspect to the hearing.

In addition, there are many situations during which predominantly oral methods of communication require the solicitor to also be adept at questioning and the non-verbal skills of prompts and listening, allied with the ability to maintain effective notes.

Where oral communication is required, it is important to maintain an awareness of both the advantages and limitations that it can bring.

On the positive side, oral communication is:

- Interpersonal
- Transparent
- Allows for high degrees of understanding
- Flexible
- Spontaneous
- Time-efficient
- An aid to problem-solving
- Allows for the use of tone, empathy, and understanding
- Promotes active engagement
- Allows for inherent confidentiality

However, it also features a number of drawbacks, including:

- A lack of formality
- Can lead to misunderstanding
- Requires a receptive and attentive audience
- Immediacy can lead to difficulty, as once a statement is said, it is out there
- Can be more time-consuming, particularly when a speech is made

1.4 A Student-Centred Approach to Skills Development

It is important to note that whilst oral communication skills can often be viewed as being an area in which an individual has strength, or perhaps does not, they are still a set of skills that can be developed and improved. Whilst there is no set of rules that applies to successful communication, it is true that each person will feel at their most comfortable when they are able to utilise a style that is natural, effective for the context, and that suits their own personality.

The following areas can assist legal professionals as they look to enhance their own communication skills:

- Reading – By expanding the amount of reading that we do, we have the effect of expanding our vocabulary, which aids in the primary purpose of communication – namely, clarity of expression.
- Be selective with your vocabulary – It is often said that legal professionals are not paid by the word. Always seek to select wording carefully to convey what is needed in as concise a way as possible. In addition, it is very easy in the law to seek to use a range of terms that are specific to those with legal training and experience, and this can be confusing and can disconnect the listener.
- Prepare and practice – The adage in legal practice is to write what is required and then read it on multiple occasions before sending the document out into

the world. A similar approach can be of great assistance as we look to develop our verbal skills. By planning what we will say, we aid understanding and our own confidence in what we are seeking to convey.

- Listening is just as important as speaking, possibly more so – When we listen, we allow our listener into the conversation and can check that we have been understood. This helps to build trust and empathy and helps to start a relationship on the correct footing.
- Do not overlook non-verbal communication – It is ever so easy to have the correct words for the context and yet fail to effectively communicate through how we say those words. It is important to always consider tone, gestures, facial expression, and body language as forming a significant part of how we communicate.
- An honest answer is better than an exaggeration – Whilst it can be tempting to wish to present yourself as the font of all knowledge, it can be more positive to an ongoing relationship to convey where you do not have an answer, rather than potentially breaking a trust at a later point if our boast was beyond our capability.
- Think about the audience perspective – Tailoring messages to fit with a wide variety of differing audiences is a key skill within the legal sector.

1.5 Finding Your Legal Voice

Perhaps the best example that we observe of legal oral communication in action is within the court environment. Here is where Solicitors, Solicitor Advocates, and Barristers take the floor and work to create a narrative that supports the relevant cause of action. When we observe peers within the court setting, it is important to observe how pitch, volume, tone, pace, and verbal mannerisms can work to enhance or reduce the standing of the individual.

Applying the concept across all aspects of legal practice shows how important it is to use vocal variety to keep an audience's attention. This could be achieved by lowering the pitch and slowing the pace to convey gravity or increasing the pitch and quickening the pace to convey excitement.

Pitch

The effective use of pitch is key to avoiding monotony in our verbal delivery. Whilst a high pitch conveys surprise, curiosity, or excitement, a lower pitch can convey seriousness, authority, or even boredom, it is these changes in pitch that are key to the effective engagement of a listener. When experienced in the use of pitch, it is possible to deliver content that maintains active listening from those in attendance. However, the incorrect use of these techniques can have adverse effects. For example, the use of a higher pitch can convey nervousness, which could lead to an interviewee having less confidence in your ability.

Volume

Volume can be a valuable tool in our armoury to convey both confidence and enthusiasm via the use of appropriate vocal projection. By using a louder volume, we can indicate a range of positions, including assertiveness, passion, or urgency. At the same time, the use of lower volume levels helps to communicate humility, intimacy, or subtlety. When we observe legal practitioners within a court setting, it is often the case that points are emphasised by a gradual raising of volume. This can then be contrasted with the use of lower volume levels to emphasise detail.

Tone

Tone is a valuable device to convey both attitude and intention. The use of a warm and friendly tone enhances views of approachability – a key requirement in a legal interview situation, where we need a client to often disclose highly personal and potentially embarrassing information. Due to this, tone should seek to match the purpose and context of the situation.

Pace

The pace at which we speak is a vital component of effective communication. Speak too fast and we convey nervousness and make our message difficult to decipher and understand. On the opposite side, a slow pattern of speech can make it challenging for the listener to maintain engagement.

Verbal Mannerisms

Lots of us have physical or verbal mannerisms that do not really matter day to day. In public speaking, however, mannerisms are magnified and can detract from our message. Common examples of verbal mannerisms can be observed every day by simply watching people being interviewed as part of news or sports broadcasts. Often, the interviewee will resort to stock filler phrases, with the classic 'erm' often being prevalent.

It is important that we regularly practice our legal communication skills through either direct experience, practice within a legal environment, or even through practice in our everyday lives with a view to ensuring that we can use the full range of possible tools to ensure that we are effective.

1.6 The Heart of Communication – The Recipient

It is a well-established aspect of legal life that even as we take our first steps in learning the law, we are greeted by a range of terms that can often be referred to as 'legalise'. Perhaps the most important distinction between legal language and the layperson, can be demonstrated by the legal profession's ongoing insistence on the use of Latin phrases within legal speech.

You may well have come across terms such as *actus reus, a priori, caveat emptor, ex gratia, habeas corpus,* or even the regular favourites of tort students, *novus actus interveniens* or *Volenti non fit injuria*. These are just some of many examples of how there are clear differences between the solicitor's everyday language and that of the client.

It is, therefore, an essential aspect of our role as legal communicators to ensure that we use all of our communication skills in a fashion that is directed towards the listener's needs, be that the client, our colleagues in either legal or non-legal roles, or perhaps even a member of the judiciary.

1.7 Clarity and Structure

It is often observed in professional life that the last person to know that their well-crafted speech on a subject did not reach the recipient as intended, is the speaker themselves. We naturally believe that what we say is understood by all, yet there are many misunderstandings that come about through a lack of clarity in our everyday interactions.

Clarity is important in communication for several reasons, as it helps to reduce misunderstanding whilst showing that you are considerate of the needs of your audience. In addition, clear communication helps to build trust and reduce conflict and the frustration that follows when a person does not know what is needed or expected.

We can aid our clarity of expression in several ways:

- Communicate appropriately to the audience.
- Use simple, plain English, and avoid unnecessary technical terms.
- Be clear and concise. It is important to be clear about what you want to say and to then say this in a manner that is concise and to the point. Speak slowly and use short sentence structures to aid understanding.
- Use examples as these can aid a recipient's understanding of the point that you are seeking to make.
- Check understanding with the use of response questions.
- Be patient and attentive to the level of the audience.
- Communicating effectively takes time, effort, and practice.

Structure is important in oral communication because, like written communication, it influences how an audience receives a message. When we can plan what we will say, for example, for a presentation or within aspects of advocacy, it is advisable to structure our message through the use of the "introduction, body, and conclusion" technique. This provides a clear purpose and allows for the listener to be led through the points being made. Of course, much of what we say is not typically planned, and we must respond quickly to what is said.

A legal interview is a great example of where we can use formal structures to plan aspects of the appointment, such as the introduction, initial questions, and the conclusion of the session. It is also advisable to use similar structures even where we are required to respond to interactions more spontaneously with a potential client.

1.8 Two-Way Communication

It is often the case that legal professionals are portrayed by their ability to speak. Thinking about any portrayal of a legal matter within popular culture will tend to lead us to consider the classic legal speeches akin to Sir Wilfrid Robarts in *Witness for the Prosecution* or perhaps Daniel Kaffee in *A Few Good Men*.

However, it is the legal professional's ability to listen and engage in two-way communication which is perhaps the more important reality of life within practice.

The *LexisNexis Bellweather Report 2015: The Age of the Client* highlighted the challenge that exists in working effectively with legal clients. The report highlighted that whilst 92% of solicitors rated themselves as being good listeners, only 67% of their clients agreed – quite a differential between expectation and delivery!

Good communication is critical to the legal professional, because before we can effectively advise, advocate, or negotiate for our clients, we need to fully understand their issues, their concerns, and their aims. It is, therefore, helpful to understand how the listening process works through consideration of the concepts of passive and active listening.

1.8.1 Active Listening

Active listening is a crucial communication skill for legal professionals as it is the key technique that allows for the building of trust, enhances understanding, and is essential to the creation of effective teams within practice.

Through the active listening process, solicitors demonstrate a genuine interest in the thoughts, feelings, and concerns of both clients and colleagues, which in turn enhances the service offered and the sense of engagement, satisfaction, and overall performance.

The techniques of active listening include:

- Giving your full attention to the speaker.
- Avoiding interruptions unless required to gain clarity.
- Paraphrasing what the speaker conveys.

- Demonstrating empathy and understanding.
- Encouraging onward open communication.

1.8.2 Passive Listening

Passive listening means listening without responding. This can be a valuable addition to the communication skills of a legal professional as it allows the solicitor to absorb the information that is being communicated. In addition, the lack of interruption and questions can often lead to a greater level of disclosure. As an example, when we leave a pause in a conversation, it is often the case that the other party will seek to fill that pause and can often disclose more than perhaps was intended.

The process of passive listening is often enhanced through the use of non-verbal cues that encourage, through action, without breaking the speakers' flow. These can include the use of eye contact, encouraging posture, surreptitious nods, or simply noises (such as 'uh huh'), all of which provide the speaker with the assurance to continue.

1.9 Leading the Narrative

Crafting key messages and forming strategic narratives are essential skills of the effective communicator. In the legal sector, regardless of whether the communication is on the telephone, in professional meetings, in the office, or in the courtroom, it is important to have a plan if we are to ensure that we achieve the required outcome from the event.

There are many aspects to consider when designing approaches to examination, cross-examination, negotiation, or client handling. One key aspect of controlling the narrative is the effective use of open and closed questions. These will be considered in greater detail in regard to interviewing in Chapter 3, but it is important at this stage to understand the terms.

1.9.1 Open Questions

Open questions are those that cannot be answered with a simple yes or no response. They require an answer where elaboration is inherent within the process.

Example questions include:

- What did he say?
- What time of day was it?
- How did you react?
- Why did you respond that way?
- Tell me more about the lead up to the accident.

1.9.2 Closed Questions

Closed questions are those that can only be answered by selecting from a limited number of options. They provide limited insight but do allow for control to be maintained within a legal setting. The classic use of these questions would be during the cross-examination of a witness.

Example questions include:

- Were you at the scene of the event?
- So, at the time, you were under the influence of the drug?
- How many drinks had you consumed?
- This was around 11pm, correct?

1.10 Non-Verbal Communication for the Legal Professional

Albert Mehrabian, a researcher into communication and specifically body language, broke down the components of face-to-face conversation and found that communication was 55% non-verbal, 38% vocal, and just 7% words. It is likely that you have observed a person telling you one version of events only for their body language to convey a very different message.

The legal professional will be required to convey often important news over the telephone, and hence it is important to work on vocal skills, but it is still the case that highly significant aspects of the role will be face-to-face with a client, a party for the other side, or a perhaps a judge. It is, therefore, vital to be aware of the important roles of appearance and body language in our communication.

1.10.1 Appearance

To underline the important role of appearance to the legal professional, it is confirmed by the SRA that candidates are required to "wear clothing suitable for a business environment" whilst completing their SQE oral assessments.

This simply requires the typical expectations of legal practice to be replicated. When a client seeks out legal advice, they are typically in a position of requiring professional expertise and knowledge. However, no matter the knowledge of the legal professional, it would be diluted if they were to attend a meeting in a pair of shorts and a Hawaiian shirt.

This is particularly important in terms of hybrid working and the use of platforms such as Teams and Zoom. Often, we will be completing meetings with clients or alternative parties to the case in front of a monitor within the comfort of our own homes. However, we must still consider our personal appearance and also the appearance of our work area – which will, of course, be visible during the meeting.

1.10.2 Body Language

Body language is a powerful tool for communicating effectively and persuasively. From the use of our hands for emphasis to our facial expressions, even our ability to make and maintain eye contact, we communicate subtle and important messages to our audience.

It is often easy to dilute a message or intention simply by distracting an audience with our own movement. Too often, when people are unsure or nervous, this is portrayed within their physical movement, with hands often being the most obvious. Hand movements can be negative and can betray thoughts, so, for example, an advocate with their hands in their pockets may appear bored or unsure of their case. It is also true to say that hand gestures at the appropriate point can emphasise a key point and leave a positive impression in the mind of the audience.

Facial expressions often give away the thoughts of the speaker. A classic example is when a verdict is issued in a case or when a witness fails to give the expected response, and it is these expressions that can leave a lasting impression with the viewer.

Eye contact, when made clearly and maintained for just the right amount of time, can be a positive aspect of submission, instilling confidence in the words that follow. However, a failure to make or maintain eye contact makes the speaker look unsure, perhaps untrustworthy, and a gaze held for too long can be uncomfortable and can raise concern.

As legal professionals, we need to be constantly aware of not just what we are saying but also how we are accompanying our words. These are skills that are always advisable to practice and to become accustomed to watching yourself in the mirror or via playback of a recording, which can aid in the control of nervous actions that you may not even be aware exist.

1.11 The Pervasive Nature of Ethics

As stated on the SRA website:

> You should note that professional conduct and ethics are core parts of SQE2 and that questions on ethics will be pervasive throughout the SQE2 assessment.

Specifically, regarding the assessment of interviewing skills, SQE2 requires that candidates:

> Conduct themselves in a professional manner and treat the client with courtesy, respect and politeness including respecting diversity where relevant.[2]

This requires that a candidate deals with matters in a sensitive manner whilst maintaining the expected standard of professionalism in their dealings with the client.

In Summary

Being Ethical

A competent legal professional should be able to:

- Follow professional rules, principles, and codes of conduct related to standards and regulations and act honestly and with integrity.
- Comply with and observe equality, diversity, and inclusion in their treatment of others.
- Understand, identify, and observe professional rules, principles, and codes of conduct in both working life and social life (where behaviours would impact life in practice).
- Recognise ethical issues and use effective judgement to solve ethical dilemmas.
- Be selfless, objective, transparent, and rational in their decision taking.
- Show an awareness of and apply professional rules, principles, and code of conduct to all matters.
- Deal with unforeseen circumstances by finding appropriate and ethical solutions.
- Avoid unethical behaviour that could lead to disciplinary proceedings.
- Resist any pressures by the client to act unethically, explain the ethical framework that legal professionals must operate under, and manage client expectations.
- Know that where professional rules and codes of conduct conflict, a legal professional should follow the one that best serves the public interest.
- Ensure that matters advised upon are within the bounds of professional competence.

Being Professional and Exercising Judgement

A competent legal professional should be able to:

- Treat clients and others with courtesy and respect, including observing equality, diversity, and inclusivity.
- Act in the client's best interests and act to achieve the client's intended objectives by assessing, analysing, and evaluating the case facts with a view to making effective judgements.
- Reflect on where and how improvements can be made, recognise when mistakes occur, and take appropriate action.

- Recognise when to seek help from others, including delegating matters beyond their expertise, seek guidance on ethical behaviours, or ask for support to solve ethical dilemmas.
- Be sensitive to the individual characteristics of others and use communication that is appropriate to the situation and takes account of the recipient.
- Use appropriate language that is not offensive and also language that is clear, succinct, and easy for clients or others to understand.
- Keep skills and knowledge up to date and take responsibility for professional learning and development.
- Manage available resources efficiently and in a way that ensures the high standards in practice that society expects of the profession and be prepared to adapt to new ways of working and new technology and development in the delivery of legal services.
- Respond promptly and appropriately to client concerns and complaints and follow internal complaints procedures.

Managing Yourself and Your Work

A competent legal professional should be able to:

- Clarify client instructions to avoid mistakes and misunderstandings.
- Use all available resources in an efficient way so that work activities can be planned and executed.
- Manage their time effectively by meeting deadlines and dealing with unforeseen circumstances as they arise.
- Keep the client informed of progress at regular intervals.
- Pay attention to details so as to ensure high standards of work and eradicate errors.

Key Practice Case

The case of *Manchester Building Society v Grant Thornton UK LLP* [2021] UKSC 20 provides a vital commentary on what constitutes negligent advice.

The matter involved Manchester Building Societies' claim that their auditors, Grant Thornton, had negligently advised them on the preparation of their accounts using a method known as 'hedge accounting'. As a result of the advice, the building society entered into a range of fixed -rate mortgages that were hedged against long-term swaps.

The hedge accounting process provided a result that obscured the true financial position of the building society as it hid the volatility of the society's capital position. Subsequently, Grant Thornton informed Manchester that the use of hedge accounting practices had been incorrect, and this led to the society having to then pay substantial costs in ending the interest rate swap contracts.

The Supreme Court found that the building society had suffered a loss that fell within the scope of the duty of care assumed by Grant Thornton in giving advice in this matter.

The panel of seven justices determined that the distinction between advice and information should not be treated as a rigid rule. They stated that the duty of care assumed by a professional should be governed by the purpose of the duty, and consideration was required of the reason why the advice had been sought.

The correct approach was therefore stated as being:

> in the case of negligent advice given by a professional adviser one looks to see what risk the duty was supposed to guard against and then looks to see whether the loss suffered represented the fruition of that risk.

Applying the law to the facts of the case, the Supreme Court ruled that the purpose of the advice from the auditors was clear:

> the society looked to Grant Thornton for technical accounting advice whether it could use hedge accounting in order to implement its proposed business model within the constraints arising by virtue of the regulatory environment, and Grant Thornton advised that it could. That advice was negligent.

This failure to advise correctly resulted in the building society suffering a loss that was directly attributable to the negligent advice.

The case is particularly important to the legal profession, where we are required to provide advice to our clients on the basis of an expert standing supported by the SRA Code of Conduct. The new simplified approach makes it more difficult for a defendant to rebut a negligence claim on the basis that they were merely providing information rather than advice.

It is now important for all those who hold themselves out as being professional in a field to ensure that the scope of the scope of the retainer/instructions is confirmed in writing between the parties so as to ensure that there is no dispute at a later point.

Practice Tips

- The process of completing a client interview is such that it is a craft that requires knowledge, experience, and training to develop the key skills of leading interpersonal communication whilst also ensuring that the client is at the heart of the interaction.
- The whole process of interviewing and advising is such that it often requires an approachable and empathetic approach that encourages dialogue. However, this has to be balanced against the need for the wide variety of roles, responsibilities, and codes of conduct to be complied with.
- If you are in doubt as to how to make an ethical decision, then reference should be made to guidance from either the professional body or from senior colleagues.

Practice Risks

- Failing to know and understand the professional rules and codes of conduct relevant to oral communication with clients.
- Failing to seek guidance and support from senior colleagues and/or the SRA on matters relating to ethical and professional conduct.
- Neglecting to consider the client's individual attributes, needs and circumstances, leading to difficulties establishing, or maintaining, the client/solicitor relationship in face to face, telephone, interview, or meeting situations.
- Poor oral communication that leads to misunderstandings or a lack of sufficient information being provided to the client.
- The potential for reputational risk from a failure to use effective communication skills with clients, the court, the defendant, or business partners.

Exercises

EXERCISE A

Refer to the SRA Standards and Regulations and consider the following problem scenario:

> It is agreed that a new sports centre will be financed with contributions made from two different finance institutions, Bowden Bank and Brown Financial.

The finance will take the form of a secured loan that will be provided by both Bowden and Brown. The two lenders have agreed that Bowden Bank will rank in priority ahead of Brown Financial, and the lenders have agreed on the form of the deed of priority.

Brown Financial has instructed you to draft the security documents. However, you have already received and accepted instructions from Bowden Bank in this matter.

Can you accept the instructions from Brown Financial?

Which rules/principles/code of conduct sections would you need to consider in order to decide how to advise Brown Financial?

EXERCISE B

Test your knowledge – MCQ's

Test one

What is the most important aspect of effective communication?

A. The sender's ability to articulate their message
B. The receiver's ability to understand the message
C. The use of complex vocabulary
D. The use of persuasive techniques
E. Asking if a person has understood the message

Test two

What is the difference between verbal and nonverbal communication?

A. Verbal communication is written, while nonverbal communication is spoken.
B. Verbal communication uses words, while nonverbal communication uses body language, facial expressions, and tone of voice.
C. Verbal communication is only used in professional settings, while nonverbal communication is used in personal settings.
D. Verbal communication is always more effective than nonverbal communication.
E. Nonverbal communication uses words, while verbal communication uses body language, facial expressions, and tone of voice.

Self-Reflection Checklist

What three important things have you learnt from this chapter?	**1**	**2**	**3**
Set out the three additional steps that you need to take to learn the skills in this chapter in more detail.	**1**	**2**	**3**

Notes

1 Solicitors Regulation Authority, 'Information You Should Expect to Receive from Your Solicitor' (*sra.org.uk*, 21 November 2024) < www.sra.org.uk/consumers/choosing/what-to-expect/> accessed 21 November 2024.

2 Solicitors Regulation Authority, 'SQE2 Assessment Specification' (*sra.org.uk*, April 2024) <https://sqe.sra.org.uk/exam-arrangements/assessment-information/sqe2-assessment-specification> accessed 21 November 2024.

2 Creating the Right Atmosphere

Key Chapter Points

1. A solicitor must meet very high professional and ethical standards, which are tested against legal and regulatory obligations.
2. In SQE2, candidates are assessed in two client interviews in the context of Property Practice and Wills and Intestacy, as well as Probate Administration and Practice.
3. In SQE2, candidates are examined pervasively on professional conduct and ethics, so the interview assessment could include a conduct issue that needs to be identified and considered.
4. Conducting an effective interview is an essential oral communication skill for every solicitor who has direct contact with clients.
5. The initial interview is one of the most important interactions with a new client, as this is when the professional client/solicitor relationship is formed.
6. Creating the right atmosphere for the initial client interview is the first and crucial stage of the interview process and begins long before the client even enters the interview room.
7. Failure to plan for the interview can affect not only the development of the client/solicitor relationship but may also impact on the outcome of the legal matter.
8. A solicitor can control the conditions for the initial interview through careful planning, and in doing so, both the client and the solicitor are able to achieve their objectives.

2.1 Introduction

This guide contains a theme which you should recognise in each chapter, which is that being a good legal professional is more than having an excellent technical understanding of legal rules and principles. A good legal professional needs to be an effective communicator, and in particular, an effective *oral* communicator, so that advice and information is communicated to clients in a clear and understandable way.

DOI: 10.4324/9781003519096-2

In Chapter 1, we considered the importance of oral communication skills to the legal profession generally. In this chapter, we focus on oral communication in the context of the initial client interview. This is probably the most important interaction a legal professional will have with a client, particularly if the client is new to the firm. Many legal professionals find interviewing challenging. This can be attributed to a combination of factors, including a lack of understanding of the pivotal role of the interview, lack of experience, failure to prepare adequately, and general uneasiness about the immediacy and uncertainty of this form of client interaction.

There are a number of reasons why the initial client interview is so important, and these are discussed later in this chapter, but it might help to pause for a moment here and remember (and to remind yourself before every initial client interview) that the person you are about to meet for the first time may be in need of help from a solicitor, but they do not need to choose *you* (or your firm) to provide this help. They can just as easily choose someone else! But they have chosen you, and this fact alone ought to be afforded due respect.

This chapter covers how to create the right atmosphere for a successful interview. By this we mean the right professional atmosphere. If you create the right professional atmosphere, you will generate an environment in which the client feels comfortable in both a physical and emotional sense. This will, in turn, enable you to form the basis of a good client/solicitor relationship, obtain the key information needed, and conduct the remainder of the legal matter effectively.

Firstly, this chapter will provide an overview of the key regulatory provisions that apply during this section of the client's journey. This information should not replace your own in-depth study of the regulatory framework that applies to solicitors. Both students and legal professionals alike must ensure that they are very well acquainted with the framework as it impacts on every element of professional practice and is tested pervasively in all of the SQE assessments.

Secondly, this chapter will take you through the basic definitions, principles, and key ingredients of client interviewing before looking at practical considerations, such as where the interview should take place, how to get the physical environment right so that it provides a welcoming and supportive space for the client and how to prepare yourself as the interviewer. Preparing yourself is important because effective interviewing can be challenging, and your role is vital to its success.

Finally, this chapter explores some of the key interpersonal skills and emotional competencies that you need to develop as a proficient interviewer so that the right emotional atmosphere is created for the interview to take place.

2.2 An Overview of the Regulatory Framework

As one would expect, the legal professions are highly regulated, and compliance with the regulatory framework is essential for maintaining ethical and professional practice.

For candidates taking the SQE2, the Solicitors Regulation Authority (SRA) specifies that professional conduct and ethics are assessed pervasively and ethical issues will not be flagged.

While a detailed discussion of the regulatory framework for solicitors and firms in England and Wales is beyond the scope of this guide, the following sections contain a brief summary of the key organisations and professional conduct rules that you need to be familiar with for client interviewing. We have also included signposts to further information so that you can continue to build on your knowledge and understanding of the regulatory structure.

2.2.1 The Legal Services Board

The Clementi Review of 2004 aimed to tackle a legal services and regulatory system which was long regarded as outdated, complex, and unaccountable. Following the Clementi Review, the framework for the regulation of legal services in England and Wales was reformed in some key areas. The Legal Services Act 2007 is the legislation that gives statutory power to the reforms.

The reforms created the Legal Services Board, which stands at the top of the hierarchy of organisations responsible for the regulation of legal professionals, including solicitors.

Under the Legal Services Act 2007, the Legal Services Board has statutory power to:

- Regulate approved regulators and the Solicitors Disciplinary Tribunal
- Oversee the Office for Legal Complaints (which is responsible for administering the Legal Ombudsman scheme)
- Make recommendations to amend the list of reserved legal activities
- Set up voluntary arrangements to improve standards (if required)

Further information about the Legal Services Board is available on its website: www.thelegalservicesboard.org.uk

2.2.2 The Law Society

The Law Society of England and Wales was founded in 1825 and is the representative body for solicitors. Until 2007, it performed both representative and regulatory functions in that it provided services and support to practising and training solicitors on the one hand AND, on the other hand, was responsible for disciplining solicitors through its regulatory department. Having a professional representative body performing the role of defence and prosecution was clearly unsatisfactory, and the Clementi Review recommended that the regulatory function of the Law Society be separated out. This function is now carried out by the Solicitors Regulation Authority.

The Law Society publishes practice notes on key areas of practice, including client care, good professional practice, and communication. The practice notes do not have legal force, but following the guidance will minimise the risks of client complaints relating to standards of service.

Further information about the role of the Law Society is available on its website: www.thelawsociety.org.uk

2.2.3 The Solicitors Regulation Authority (SRA)

The SRA, established in 2007, is the *independent* regulatory arm of the Law Society. It is tasked with protecting the public by setting standards, drafting professional conduct rules, and providing guidance on how solicitors are expected to behave.

The rules and regulations are collectively referred to as the SRA Standards and Regulations (STAR). The SRA has statutory authority under section 28 of the Legal Services Act 2007 to discharge its regulatory functions of:

1. Serving the public interest and protecting consumers of legal services; and
2. Maintaining the public's confidence in the reputation of the solicitors' profession for honesty, probity, trustworthiness, independence and integrity.

SRA Mandatory Principles

At the heart of the SRAs regulatory enforcement are the mandatory Principles.

The SRA describes the Principles as the "fundamental tenets of ethical behaviour that we expect all those that we regulate to uphold".

Those who are regulated include all those that the SRA authorises to provide legal services, and these are solicitors, registered European Lawyers (RELs) and registered foreign lawyers (RFLs), authorised firms, managers, and employees.

It is important to understand that reference to 'employees' includes non-qualified staff, for example, paralegals and legal assistants.

The Principles are set out in Table 2.1.

Here is a link to the Principles on the SRA website:

https://www.sra.org.uk/solicitors/standards-regulations/principles/

Table 2.1 SRA Principles

Principle Number	Content
1	You act in a way that upholds the rule of law and the proper administration of justice.
2	You act in a way that upholds public trust and confidence in the solicitors' profession and in legal services provided by authorised persons.
3	You act with independence.
4	You act with honesty.
5	You act with integrity.
6	You act in a way that encourages equality, diversity, and inclusion.
7	You act in the best interests of each client.

SRA Code of Conduct for Solicitors (CCS) and Code of Conduct for Firms (CCF)

The SRA sets the standards of professionalism required of those who are regulated by producing Codes of Conduct. The Code of Conduct for Solicitors (CCS) applies to solicitors, registered European lawyers (RELs), and registered foreign lawyers (RFLs), and the Code of Conduct for Firms (CCF) applies to managers and employees.

The core areas of the Codes are:

- Maintaining trust and acting fairly
- Service and competence
- Client money and assets
- Conflicts of interest
- Confidentiality and disclosure

The full text of the Codes can be found on the SRA website:

https://www.sra.org.uk/solicitors/standards-regulations/code-conduct-solicitors/
https://www.sra.org.uk/solicitors/standards-regulations/code-conduct-firms/

Breaking the Rules

Reports or complaints concerning potential professional misconduct or breaches of the Codes are assessed in the first instance by the SRA, which then decides if an investigation is needed, using a three-stage test as follows:

1. Has there been a potential breach of the SRA standards or requirements based on the allegation?

2. Is the breach sufficiently serious that, if proved, it is capable of regulatory action?
3. Is the breach capable of proof?

In its guidance *'If we are investigating you'* (available here: https://www.sra.org.uk/solicitors/guidance/investigating-you/), the SRA reports that, reassuringly, the vast majority of investigations are closed without taking further action. In cases where the SRA upholds a serious breach of the rules, the following sanctions can be imposed on the solicitor or firm:

- Written rebuke
- Financial penalty (up to £25,000)
- Disqualification
- Order to control activities
- Conditions on the practising certificate
- Revoked or suspended authorisation to practice under the SRA Authorisation of Firms Rules
- Fixed financial penalty (for non-complex breaches)
- Application to the Solicitors Disciplinary Tribunal

It is possible to request a review of an SRA decision relating to regulatory and disciplinary matters, and there is a right of appeal to the Solicitors Disciplinary Tribunal with respect to some decisions.

Further information on the role of the SRA can be accessed from its website: www.sra.org.uk

2.2.4 The Solicitors Disciplinary Tribunal (SDT)

The SDT is an independent statutory tribunal constituted under section 46 of the Solicitors Act 1974. In addition to having the authority to impose sanctions itself, under section 47 of the Solicitors Act 1974, the SRA can make an application to the SDT for an allegation of misconduct or breach of the code of conduct to be considered. The SRA then takes over the role of prosecutor of the alleged misconduct or breach before the SDT.

An application to the SDT will only be made where the SRA is satisfied that:

1. There is a realistic prospect of the Tribunal making an order in respect of the allegation; and
2. It is in the public interest to make the application.

The proceedings are governed by the Solicitors (Disciplinary Proceedings) Rules 2019, and under this statutory instrument, the SDT must deal with cases justly and at proportionate cost. On its website, the SDT states that factors that determine whether a case is referred to the SDT include the likely sanction and the nature and motivating factors of the offending misconduct itself.

The sanctions available to the SDT under section 47 of the Solicitors Act 1974 are:

- Indefinite suspension
- Fixed period suspension
- Permanent strike off the Roll of Solicitors
- Unlimited fine

Further information on the role of the SDT can be accessed from its website: www.solicitorstribunal.org.uk

2.2.5 The Legal Ombudsman for England and Wales (LeO)

The LeO was set up in 2010 by the Office for Legal Complaints under the Legal Services Act 2007 to resolve disputes between consumers and legal services providers.

Whereas the SRA and SDT deal with issues of solicitor misconduct, the LeO handles complaints about all legal service providers (including solicitors) in relation to legal services received by consumers. This is not the same as misconduct. Instead it is about poor standards of service, which does not necessarily mean a breach of the SRA rules, although it is possible for there to be both a service standard complaint and misconduct/breach of the rules. Consider the following scenarios:

Scenario 1

In an employment case, a client is mistakenly advised about a time limit to lodge an application, which is incorrect, resulting in the application being issued out of time and being rejected. This is an error relating to the ***quality of the service*** provided and could be the subject of a complaint to the Legal Ombudsman.

Scenario 2

In an employment case, a client provides information for the solicitor to submit an application. The solicitor fails to submit the application by the deadline, and the application is rejected. The solicitor dishonestly informs the client that the application was submitted on time but that it was rejected. This would be a ***conduct issue*** and could be the subject of a complaint to the SRA in relation to breach of Principles 2, 4, and 5 and Paragraph 1.4 of the CCS (maintaining trust and acting fairly).

There is a link between the work of the SRA and the LeO in the form of an operational protocol between these organisations, under which the LeO can refer possible misconduct cases to the SRA.

The LeO states that the most common complaints from consumers relate to unclear costs explanations, delay (with no clear reason), and poor information, in particular, failure to explain processes properly or providing information which is not sufficient for the client to make an informed choice.

Under Paragraph 8.2 of the CCS, solicitors must have a procedure for handling complaints from clients in relation to the legal services provided. In the first instance, the client should complain to the firm. If the issue is not resolved within eight weeks from the date of the complaint, the client should be informed in writing of their right to complain to the LeO.

If the LeO accepts a complaint relating to a solicitor, it will try to resolve the issue informally, if appropriate, or it can hold an investigation. The complaint can be determined with or without a hearing. The parties and the SRA are sent a determination with a time limit for the complainant to respond. Once the complainant accepts or rejects the determination or fails to respond, the solicitor and the SRA are notified. The solicitor/firm can be told to:

- Apologise;
- Give back any documents the client needs;
- Do more work to put right what went wrong and pay for the work;
- Refund or reduce legal fees; or,
- Pay compensation if there is a finding that the client has lost out or been badly treated (most of the awards are under £1,000).

If the complainant accepts the determination, then it becomes binding on the parties and is final. This precludes a complainant from bringing a negligence action. If the solicitor fails to carry out the actions, the complainant can enforce through the High Court. There is also a judicial review process.

Further information about the role of the LeO can be found on its website: www.legalombudsman.org.uk

2.3 Principles of Legal Interviewing

The guidance in this section of the chapter is intended to help you prepare specifically for an initial client interview, whether that be in practice or as part of your preparation for SQE2. You will see that throughout the following chapters, we have used the term 'solicitor' when discussing the person who is conducting the interview with a client. We do appreciate that solicitors are not the only legal professionals involved in interviewing clients, but we use it here for conciseness.

Although not explicitly mentioned in the SQE2 Interviewing assessment specifications, it is in the context of the *initial* client interview (as opposed to other client interviews that may take place during the life of a legal matter) that interviewing skills are assessed. Having an assessment built around an initial client interview enables candidates to demonstrate the key competencies that are relevant to the skill of interviewing, and this format replicates the Qualified Lawyers Transfer Scheme (QLTS) assessment on which the SQE is modelled.

Many of the interviewing strategies that follow in this section can be applied or adapted to suit other interviews that take place in legal practice, for example, with clients at later stages of their legal case, or perhaps in the lead-up to a trial or with witnesses. They can also be used for other professional interviews outside the legal profession, as many of the underlying structures are the same or very similar.

However, while there are factors that are common to all types of interviews (for example, a logical structure, a warm and courteous greeting, an appropriate interview environment, and the ability to build rapport and show empathy), there are also some important distinctions to be aware of. For example, as a solicitor, the professional relationship that you will form with a client is likely to be much more challenging in terms of your time and emotional commitment than, for example, the relationship with a witness in a case.

Additionally, the professional conduct obligations that apply to the legal profession are not replicated in other industries. It is crucial that a solicitor can demonstrate, within an initial interview, that these obligations have been met.

In the next section, we will consider the main principles that apply to legal interviewing. Some of this information may seem obvious, but you may find it useful to refresh your memory and ensure you have a sound understanding of the foundations of interviewing before turning to how the interview environment can be controlled.

2.3.1 What Is the Initial Client Interview?

An interview differs from other forms of oral communication, such as informal conversations. These usually feel very natural or intuitive and do not require preparation. Conversations, for example, with a friend or family member, often begin and end spontaneously with no specific goal in mind. An interview is different because it is a meeting with a particular goal. For example, taking part in a job interview is a standard part of a recruitment process, with the main purpose being to secure employment/fill a vacancy. Another example is a potential student hoping to secure a place at a preferred university through an interview process.

A legal client interview has a number of purposes. In its guidance, the Law Society describes the interview as an opportunity to discuss a client's legal needs, what the practice will be able to offer, and the likely costs. This is a useful starting point, but it offers no information about other perhaps less obvious but nonetheless vital purposes, including building rapport, trust, and confidence.

An initial client interview, if all goes to plan, is when the client/solicitor relationship is formed. It is an opportunity for mutual assessment, after which time, the matter may or may not continue. It is a personal interaction between a potential client and a legal professional, which is happening in a professional context. As it involves two strangers, it is an interaction that both parties may find emotionally challenging. It could perhaps be likened to a first date, with either one or both parties experiencing a mixture of hope, nervousness, uncertainty, and possibly also dread!

A client may have little or no previous experience with the legal profession and may be unsure what to expect. There may be underlying anxieties caused by the legal issue itself, and added to that, the meeting may be taking place on unfamiliar territory. Perceptions and emotions vary widely from person to person, and one client may find the experience intensely stressful and intimidating, while another may already have some experience of the legal profession and perhaps more emotional resilience.

For a solicitor, an initial interview can be a step into the unknown and may require emotional input capable of pushing them out of their comfort zone. A new client is a stranger, and the interaction may present unique challenges and outcomes which could not have been anticipated, even with careful planning.

2.3.2 Is Effective Interviewing an Aptitude or a Skill?

Is the ability to interview effectively an aptitude or a skill? An aptitude is natural ability, whereas a skill is something that is capable of being developed. Being an effective interviewer relies on being an effective communicator. While some people give the impression of being naturally good communicators, others feel that this is something that they do not do well. However, communicating effectively can be considered a skill (not an aptitude), so those who believe they do not do it well should feel confident that they can learn and develop this skill. This in turn will assist in becoming an effective interviewer.

It is understandable that the prospect of conducting either a real or even a simulated interview makes many students and less experienced legal professionals feel very nervous. However, with a solid theoretical foundation, plenty of practice, and a willingness to critically reflect, becoming a confident and effective interviewer is very achievable.

2.3.3 Why Is Interviewing Important?

The oral communication skills that are relevant in legal practice and which are reflected in assessments at SQE2 are interviewing, advocacy, and negotiation. While there is no separate assessment for negotiation, it may make an appearance in interviewing and attendance note/legal analysis and/or in the written skills assessment of case and matter analysis and/or legal writing.

Of course, advocacy, interviewing, and negotiating are not the only forms of oral communication that we encounter as legal professionals. There will be many occasions throughout the working day when the solicitor is communicating either formally or informally with colleagues and other professionals, and this in itself is an important skill (not to be underestimated) in forming strong professional relationships with those we work with.

Clearly, advocacy and the art of persuasion are essential skills for those wishing to specialise in contentious areas of practice requiring advocacy in the lower courts and for those with higher rights of audience. Negotiation, too, is an integral part of a legal professional's skill set. The skills involved in advocacy and negotiation do overlap to some extent with interviewing in relation to some of the techniques used, namely active listening and questioning, but they also involve skills that are not used in interviewing, for example, the ability to influence and persuade. There are skills that are unique to interviewing, which are not used as regularly in advocacy or negotiation (although this depends on the context). An important example is the formulating and giving of on-the-spot advice which often happens during an interview.

The importance of interviewing in the range of oral communication skills lies in the extent of its use in practice. This is very broad indeed, much more so than either advocacy or negotiating. Most new entrants to the profession are likely to spend a significant amount of their time engaged in interviewing because, in theory, at least, each new client to a firm should be offered an initial interview.

This is not to say that one form of oral communication is more valuable than the other. They all have equal standing in the different contexts in which they are used. But, the successful presentation of a client's case within a court environment and the ability to negotiate effectively are skills which are *developed* from the foundational oral communication skills acquired through interviewing. It is the skill of interviewing that is usually learned first, and the client interview is the most frequently occurring context in which legal professionals will communicate verbally with a client.

It is difficult to see how a legal professional can progress onto the skills of negotiating or advocacy if they have not mastered the basics of interviewing, so it is essential for students and legal professionals alike to ensure that they acquire these foundational skills and apply them competently in practice, to the high professional standards required.

2.3.4 Why Is the *Initial* Client Interview So Important?

From a commercial perspective, the initial client interview is arguably the most crucial step in the process of acquiring and retaining new clients, so it is vital that it is conducted properly. A successful interview is simply very good for business. If done effectively, a good client/solicitor relationship will be formed, and this will usually result in the potential client formally instructing the firm to act for them in the matter and probably also in other matters. A happy client is also a very useful client when it comes to good publicity. Word of mouth is still an important way of acquiring new clients, and in an era of consumer power, positive and negative online reviews can have a huge impact on business.

If, on the other hand, the interview is conducted unsuccessfully and the client is dissatisfied, there is a risk that the client's journey with the firm will end here and will not progress to the formal instructions stage. The lost client will instead seek out a solicitor who they feel they can trust with their legal matter.

An important reminder of the changing landscape of legal services and the power of the client is contained in the introduction to the *LexisNexis Bellwether Report of 2015: The Age of the Client* (page 4), which we referred to in Chapter 1. We mention it again here because it neatly sums up the position as follows:

> A new breed of smart client has emerged – empowered by technology and the internet, always searching for the best value, and very much aware of their own importance as customers.

The message about the dynamics of the relationship between a client and a solicitor could not be clearer. Clients wield a great deal of power, and firms have to develop their services accordingly.

The initial interview is the event when relevant and accurate information is obtained about the legal matter. It is not the only time that information can be obtained, but there are a couple of points to note. Firstly, the solicitor will lose credibility if they have not asked questions that should have been asked at the initial meeting. This also wastes time, as the solicitor must then go back to the client to fill in the gaps. Secondly, information gathered from the initial meeting could very swiftly set in motion a chain of events that influences the direction of the case, for example, an emergency application in a family law matter or urgently issuing a claim form to protect a limitation period in a personal injury matter.

If the solicitor has not used effective communication and key information is missing or misunderstood, this may have a detrimental impact on the client/solicitor relationship and the case itself. This could result in a formal complaint and/or a professional negligence claim against the solicitor.

If done effectively, the initial meeting enables the solicitor to showcase excellent client care from the outset, and this is a key factor in client satisfaction and retention.

2.3.5 The Aims and Objectives of the Initial Client Interview

The broad aim of the initial client interview is uncomplicated. Clients engage the services of solicitors because they have a legal problem or transaction that they need help with, and the initial interview is the first stage in receiving that help. This is mirrored by what the solicitor ultimately wants from the meeting, which is to help the client with a legal problem or transaction and to do so in a manner which is in the client's best interests.

If we break down the aim into client/solicitor interview objectives, it might look something like this:

1. Build a rapport with the client to enable a professional relationship to be formed
2. Find out why the client has come and identify the legal issue
3. Identify and understand the client's goals relating to the legal issue
4. Gather relevant information
5. Give explanations and advice if appropriate
6. Help the client make an informed decision
6. Agree a plan for future action or basic steps to move the matter forward
7. Deal with client care and costs information

Each of the objectives will involve the solicitor employing a range of skills and competencies.

2.3.6 What Skills and Competencies Are Needed?

To meet the objectives (and meet the aim), the solicitor needs to use a range of professional and practical skills effectively.

The skills required are:

- Listening
- Questioning
- Analysing
- Explaining
- Advising
- Note taking

The solicitor must also use social and interpersonal skills which can be referred to as emotional competencies. The emotional competencies include:

- Being able to build rapport
- Being able to build trust and confidence
- Being aware of barriers to communication and working to minimise them
- Being able to build communication bridges
- Being able to empathise

2.3.7 The Structure of the Initial Client Interview

As the meeting is a professional one, a degree of formality in terms of observance of etiquette and an appropriate meeting structure should be considered. The interview should not begin with the interviewer turning up unprepared, late, and slurping a coffee. This will instantly give a client the impression of someone who is disorganised and unprofessional. On the other hand, the meeting should not be so formal and structured as to inhibit effective communication. The consequence of too much or too little formality and structure will be that the client does not feel comfortable enough to speak openly.

There are no hard and fast rules about the structure of an initial client interview as long as the objectives are being met in a logical way and in a manner that prevents the interview from drifting. Without any structure, before you know it, you have been talking to a client for much of the diary time set aside for the meeting, but without actually having achieved the key interview objectives.

At the very least, there should be a distinct beginning, middle, and end to the interview. This will make it much easier to meet the objectives at 2.3.4.

You might already have a structure that you use, but if not, you may find the following useful:

Phase 1 (preliminary matters)

- Meet, greet, and seat
- Ice breaker
- Establish the reason for the client's appointment
- Outline the structure of the interview
- Client care matters

Phase 2 (listening)

- Elicit client's story with an opening question
- Listen carefully using active and passive listening techniques

Phase 3 (questioning)

- Fill in the gaps using a range of questioning techniques
- Summarise the solicitor's understanding of the facts
- Check for the client's agreement of the solicitor's understanding and amend if necessary

Phase 4 (explaining and advising)

- Explain legal position and relevant law/procedure
- State options/advice to achieve the client's objectives
- Help the client reach a decision
- Agree on a plan of action

Phase 5 (closing)

- Establish whether the client wishes to proceed with instructions
- Repeat advice/plan of action and check for client's agreement
- Confirm follow-up work for both parties
- Check for understanding of risks
- Check for an understanding of costs

- State the next contact between the parties
- Any other questions
- Terminate and goodbye

2.3.8 A Client-Centred Approach to Interviewing

There has been much debate in recent years about the dynamics of the solicitor/client relationship. It was traditionally viewed as a paternalistic relationship involving very little client participation. Medicine was the first profession to turn the lens inwards on its own practices. In the 1950s and 60s, the traditional patient/doctor relationship, where patients were passive and followed medical advice without question, was identified as problematic. The upshot was a cultural shift to more patient-centred care. This can be seen in the development of the principles of patient autonomy and informed consent.

The legal profession has lagged behind the medical profession somewhat, but it is now widely accepted in legal practice, too, that a more collaborative approach, where client participation and empowerment are encouraged, is more beneficial for clients in terms of matter outcome and client satisfaction.

In essence, being client-centred is about sensitivity to and understanding of a person as an individual, not just in the context of a legal problem that needs to be solved. We must be client-centred during all stages of the client's journey, including the planning stage of the initial interview. A client-centred approach is at the heart of ethical and modern lawyering, and a client-centred law firm is one that puts its clients at the centre of its thinking and planning.

2.3.9 A Client-Centred Approach in SQE2

The focus of legal education was traditionally on technical knowledge of the law with little emphasis on skills training. In the 1970s, the clinical and skills movements laid the foundations for the integration of skills into the vocational stage of legal education, and if we fast forward to 1993, the Legal Practice Course was launched and included assessment of a range of skills, including interviewing. Candidates now taking the SQE2 assessment will in addition need to demonstrate a client-focus in their approach to interviewing.

The skills and ethical principles of interviewing, using a client-centred approach, are explicitly and firmly embedded in the SQE2 assessment criteria.

The indicators demonstrating competence/non-competence for a client-focused approach are:

- The candidate demonstrates an understanding of the client's problem from the client's perspective (e.g., the candidate addresses the client's legal

problem, any relevant commercial considerations, and/or the client's personal circumstances).
- The candidate acknowledges and responds to the client's concerns with interest and empathy.

The indicators that do not demonstrate competence are:

- The candidate does not approach or appreciate the client's problem from the client's perspective.
- The candidate does not respond to the client's concerns with interest and empathy.
- The candidate provides advice which does not take into account the client's aims or concerns.

The full performance indicators for SQE2 Interviewing can be accessed here:

https://sqe.sra.org.uk/docs/default-source/pdfs/sqe2-sample-questions/int-performance-indicators.pdf?sfvrsn=69961d98_2

2.4 Controlling the Interview Environment

This purpose of this section is to provide guidance on the practical steps to create the right atmosphere for the interview to take place. Control is an awkward word to use directly after a paragraph about being client-centred, but the intention is not to use it in a negative sense to mean the domination of a client, by the solicitor, but rather to highlight the importance of planning, with the individual client in mind.

There may, of course, be aspects of an interview that we have no control over (such as where it takes place in the offices of the firm), but the general advice is that we should plan for all aspects of the interview that are within our control. Consider the other key oral skill of advocacy and whether you think it would be acceptable for an advocate to turn up to court without having prepared and planned for a hearing. Clearly, that would not be an acceptable way to perform the role of advocate. In the same way, it is not acceptable to conduct an initial interview without planning and preparing for it.

The issue of control is specifically referred to in the SQE2 interview assessment. Candidates need to be able to:

> Conduct themselves in a professional manner and treat the client with courtesy, respect, and politeness, including respecting diversity where relevant.

The indicators demonstrating competence are:

- The candidate maintains control of the interview (e.g., the candidate is well organised, calm, composed, and efficient and does not appear rushed).

The indicators that do not demonstrate competence are:

- The candidate is hesitant throughout or lacking in confidence, appears rushed and flustered, and is not in control of the interview.

The full performance indicators for SQE2 Interviewing can be accessed here:

https://sqe.sra.org.uk/docs/default-source/pdfs/sqe2-sample-questions/int-performance-indicators.pdf?sfvrsn=69961d98_2

Being well-organised, calm, composed, and efficient will enable the solicitor to create the atmosphere needed to establish a solid professional relationship with the client. Taking this approach also enables the solicitor to conduct the interview ethically and in compliance with the relevant professional conduct rules.

2.4.1 Where Should the Initial Client Interview Take Place?

The reality of modern legal practice (alongside most professions) is that the initial client interview and many other client interactions will not necessarily take place at the firm's offices, as might traditionally have been the case. Advances in technology and adjustments in working patterns largely brought about as a consequence of the Covid-19 pandemic lockdowns in 2020 have inevitably led to more dynamic and varied working environments.

In some firms, initial interviews may not take place at all, having been replaced entirely by digital processes, or firms may have a policy of only taking initial instructions by telephone or via video conference. If the firm does offer in-person appointments to clients, these may not necessarily take place in the solicitor's office but may happen at the client's home or at a location off- site.

Following the pandemic, many firms continue to operate a hybrid working model and have no plans to return to a requirement of full-time office attendance. Office space has been down sized with the knock-on effect that many firms simply no longer have the office facilities to accommodate in-person appointments. Meeting clients over Teams or Zoom saves the firm time and money and, for those very reasons, is often the preferred option for clients.

While many of the principles of effective interviewing can be applied to all interview settings, whether in-person, by video call, or by telephone, this guide is primarily concerned with the in-person initial interview that takes place at the offices of the solicitor. This is because conducting the initial client interview in person is by far the most effective way to cement the client/solicitor relationship, and it is this form of interview that is simulated in the SQE 2 interviewing assessment.

Whichever setting a firm decides to use for an initial interview, there are some key points to note:

- The interview should take place in an environment that maximises communication and reduces barriers.
- In-person interviews allow for non-verbal communication and cues to be picked up whereas other methods do not allow this to the same degree (there is a risk in a digital or telephone appointment of missing body language, facial expressions, or vocal cues that would have been revealed in person).
- Particular care needs to be taken when obtaining initial instructions in certain practice areas, for example, wills drafting and property transactions, to rule out undue influence.
- The venue for an interview may be dependent on a number of regulatory and ethical factors, including the potential vulnerability of a client and individual attributes, needs and circumstances.

Although there are clearly some practical advantages for both parties to having a remote interview (and the client may indicate that this is their preferred option), it is recognised that a face-to-face, in-person interview at the firm's offices is best practice (subject to an assessment of a client's potential vulnerability and individual attributes, needs and circumstances which are considered later in this chapter) and it should be accommodated wherever possible.

2.4.2 Ethical Considerations at the Planning Stage of the Interview

The following sections explain the legal and professional conduct considerations specific to the planning stage of the interview.

2.4.2.1 The Equality Act 2010

Under the Equality Act 2010, solicitors and firms are legally obligated to provide reasonable adjustments to disabled clients and others. The SRA also states that the expectations extend beyond the minimum legal standards as set out in the Equality Act 2010, and there is a duty to take positive steps for disabled clients and employees.

2.4.2.2 SRA Principles and Codes of Conduct (CCS and CCF)

- **Principle 6 – you act in a way that encourages equality, diversity, and inclusion**

This duty extends to potential clients and the first interview. The duty is to ensure that people are treated fairly and are offered the same rights and opportunities. Principle 6 is supplemented by CCS 1.1, which states that you do not unfairly discriminate by allowing your personal views to affect your professional relationships and the way services are provided.

- **Principle 7 – you act in the best interests of each client**

The overarching provision when planning the initial client interview and which you need to be familiar with is Principle 7, which requires you to act in the best interests of each client. This includes prospective and former clients. When arranging an interview, this will involve consideration of the following:

- Conflict of interest
- Confidentiality
- Expertise
- Capacity

- **CCS 3.1 and CCF 4.1** – **you act only on instructions from the client or from someone who is properly authorised to provide instructions on their behalf**

CCS 3.1 and the corresponding provision CCF 4.1 set the minimum service standard required, which is that the solicitor/firm only acts on instructions from the client or from someone who is properly authorised to provide instructions on their behalf.

Acting on instructions from a person who is not authorised by the client to give instructions on their behalf will be a breach of the Code and is evidence that Principle 7 has not been upheld. The importance the SRA places on these sections of the Codes means that firms need to ensure that their procedures for taking on new clients are watertight.

The requirement when taking the client's instructions is to ensure that:

- They are the instructions of the client;
- If they are not received directly from the client, the person providing instructions is properly authorised to do so;
- Where there are suspicions that something is not right, time is taken to investigate fully;
- Where it is not possible to be sure about whether they are the instructions of the client, but it appears that they are, the best interests of the client are protected.

Solicitors need to be sure not only that the instructions are coming from the person purporting to be the client but that the client is who they say they are. This is particularly relevant to fraud in conveyancing transactions and is specifically addressed in the Law Society's Conveyancing Quality Scheme (CQS), which provides at 5.13 of its core practice management standards that firms must:

> have a policy in relation to the avoidance of involvement in property and mortgage fraud, which must include (e) a procedure for enhanced checking of the identity (and retaining full records of such identity) of the practice's client in transactions where a high risk of fraud is present.

Further details of the CQS are available here:
https://www.lawsociety.org.uk/topics/firm-accreditations/conveyancing-quality-scheme

- **CCS 3.4 and CCF 4.2 – you consider and take account of your client's attributes, needs, and circumstances**

CCS 3.4 CCS and CCF 4.2 require solicitors and firms to take into account a client's attributes, needs, and circumstances. This is acknowledging, on a regulatory level, that each client is unique and must be treated as an individual. This will be most relevant when acting for a vulnerable client or a client who lacks mental capacity, but its application is, in fact, much wider, as you will see from 2.4.2.3 and **Table 2.2.**

- **CCS 6.3 and CCF 6.3 – you keep the affairs of current and former clients confidential unless disclosure is required or permitted by law or the client consents**

A solicitor will have to be mindful of the duty contained in CCS/CCF 6.3, which requires that a client's affairs are kept confidential unless required or permitted by law or the client consents. One of the most important considerations for the client during an interview is privacy. Whether it's a medical consultation or an interview in a law firm, people generally do not want to share their private affairs with people outside the consultation/interview room. The requirement to ensure confidentiality of information is a regulatory one, and it needs to be considered when selecting the venue for the interview.

Please also refer to the following link:
https://www.sra.org.uk/solicitors/standards-regulations/code-conduct-solicitors/

- **STEP Code for Will Preparation in England and Wales (STEP 2016)**

The Society of Trust and Estate Practitioners (STEP) is a global professional organisation which sets standards for inheritance and succession planning. Legal professionals who prepare wills and who are members of STEP must adhere to the STEP Code, which is an additional set of ethical principles of best practice that underpin wills drafting.

Code 4 (iv) states:

> When taking instructions from a client the will drafter must endeavour to ensure that no member of the testator's family, or an intended beneficiary under the will, is present during the meeting. It is understood that in some circumstances this may not be possible, and if the will drafter feels able to proceed with the interview they must:
>
> a. provide a careful explanation of the potential for challenge to the terms of the will; and
> b. take careful note of the third party's participation in the meeting in order to assist with any later dispute.

Further information on STEP can be accessed here:

https://www.step.org/

2.4.2.3 Areas of Concern in Practice

The SRA acknowledges that there are particular areas of concern in practice relating to vulnerable clients, mental capacity, and undue influence. These areas of concern are interlinked and often go hand in hand. Be mindful, for example, that if a person's mental capacity is in question, not only will this suggest that a client is vulnerable, but it may also make them susceptible to undue influence, and a client who is being unduly influenced may be classed as vulnerable because of it (although they may not lack mental capacity).

We will look at each area in turn:

Vulnerable Clients

A solicitor needs to be aware of the obligations relating to vulnerable clients and the issues to consider before accepting instructions. A statutory definition of 'vulnerable adult' is contained in the Care Act 2014 and includes people over 18 to whom the state has specific safeguarding responsibilities, for example, if they are in sheltered accommodation or have a social worker. However, 'vulnerable client' is much wider than the statutory definition of 'vulnerable adult', and a solicitor must consider a broader range of characteristics and situations when determining if a client is vulnerable.

There is not an exhaustive list of characteristics and situations, but a solicitor should be mindful of the following factors in **Table 2.2** when considering whether a client is vulnerable:

Table 2.2 Factors when considering if a client is vulnerable or not

Characteristics	Situations
Age	Bereavement
Low income	Threat of harm
Inexperience	Loss of income
Low literacy	Victim of crime
Physical disability	Victim of accident
Health problems	Loss of employment
Learning disability	Relationship breakdown
Mental health issues	Recently left care
English as a second language	Recently left prison
Cultural barriers	Threat of deportation
Being a carer	Concern over access to children
Lone parent	Concern over child welfare

The SRA recognises that if a person is vulnerable, then receiving a poor service has an even more serious impact than if the person is not vulnerable. Vulnerable clients are entitled to a proper level of legal service, and solicitors must ensure that this is the standard of service received. This means that a solicitor must respond to individual vulnerabilities by tailoring the interview to them.

Undue Influence

Undue influence arises when the relationship between two people is being exploited by one person to gain an unfair advantage over the other person. Great care needs to be taken by legal professionals, particularly when conducting private client work involving estate and financial planning, property transactions, and wills. A client may indicate that they want a family member, friend, or carer to attend an interview with them. People may genuinely want to help their loved ones for the best of intentions, and the client may have consented to this, but a solicitor must be mindful of the possibility of conflicts of interest or undue influence if someone else is helping a client.

If a solicitor assesses that a client has capacity, they should be seen on their own so that instructions can be confirmed directly with them. A client may wish to see a solicitor because they have been put under pressure to do so. It can be a fine line between a well-intentioned relative who is genuinely trying to help and undue influence, but if a solicitor has suspicions that a client's instructions are the result of undue influence, it will not be possible to act unless the solicitor is satisfied that the instructions are genuinely the client's wishes.

Mental Capacity

Mental capacity is the ability to make a particular decision and is decision-specific, so a client could have the capacity to make a decision about where to live but lacks the capacity to make the necessary financial arrangements. Mental capacity is not static and may fluctuate, so a client may initially have capacity but subsequently lose capacity, and vice versa.

Paragraph 3.4 CCS covers the issue of capacity. If a solicitor has reasonable doubt about a client's capacity to give instructions, they must satisfy themselves whether the client has the capacity to give those instructions. There are different tests depending on the type of legal matter, a detailed discussion of which is beyond the scope of this guide, but more information can be accessed from the Law Society website:

https://www.lawsociety.org.uk/topics/client-care/working-with-clients-who-may-lack-mental-capacity

2.4.3 Planning for the Arrival of the Client

In The Hobbit, Gandalf warns of the dangers of ignoring a live dragon if it lives nearby (Tolkien, 1993, p. 217). In other words, planning is the best way to avoid disaster! Generally, in life, whether it is preparing a simple meal or building a house, a plan reduces uncertainty, gives a sense of direction, and makes it much easier to achieve the desired goal! Interviews are no different, and the first important part of the interview is to plan for it.

The following sections provide guidance on how to plan and prepare for an initial client interview which is taking place at the offices of the firm, although it may be that in taking account of your client's attributes, needs, and circumstances (CCS 3.4), you decide that it is more appropriate for the initial interview to take place elsewhere, for example at the client's home.

We will consider in detail the importance of first impressions when discussing how to build rapport in section 2.4, but it should be appreciated that the very first impression that the client will form, even before meeting the solicitor, is on entering the doors of the firm's offices.

The first contact for a client will usually be with the reception staff, who should provide basic information such as an indication of how long they are likely to have to wait (but please note that you should avoid keeping clients waiting unless unavoidable); the location of the toilets and an offer of refreshment. The reception area itself should be clean and comfortable. The objective here is to ensure that the client's physical and emotional well-being is being attended to from the outset so that when you meet the client, they are as relaxed as possible and have already started to feel a sense of trust and confidence in the firm.

Make sure that if you need an independent language or sign language interpreter, this has been arranged and that you have set aside some time before the interview to meet the interpreter and discuss issues such as confidentiality.

2.4.4 Preparing the Interview Room

Part of the preparation for the interview is to check the interview room. Again, this might seem obvious, but it is nevertheless worthy of a mention, as it is a stage in the planning that can be easily overlooked in the busy working day of the solicitor who has a full diary and countless tasks all competing for attention. This is not to say that a solicitor should go about preparing the interview room in the mode of an interior decorator, spending hours arranging and re-arranging furniture, pictures, and potted plants!

If interviews take place in a designated interview or conference room within the offices, then you may not have to do anything other than a quick check to make sure there is everything you and the client will need. If you do have direct control over the interview environment, for example, if it is your own office, you will need to think about what a client's minimum expectations would be.

2.4.4.1 Minimum Expectations for an Interview Room

The interview room should, at the very least, provide:

- A safe, clean, and comfortable room free from obstructions and potential hazards
- A private space where conversations cannot be overheard either by staff or other clients (and where you and the client cannot overhear the conversations of others)
- A room which is not facing a corridor/window where people are continuously passing during the interview
- A room with no physical barriers (e.g., files/folders piled high) to hinder communication
- A room with a seating/table arrangement that is comfortable for both parties and allows for the client to make notes (see what follows for further information)

The interview should not take place in an open-plan space. If sharing an office, arrangements should be made for colleague/colleagues to vacate the room for the duration of the interview.

2.4.4.2 Seating and Table Arrangements

There is no consensus on the most effective arrangement of chairs and tables, and much will depend on the firm's office facilities and layout. A client might feel uncomfortable under the glare of a solicitor across a large conference table, and the distance between the parties may create barriers, so if the interview is to take place in a designated conference room, think about the best position for the chairs.

Seating may need to vary depending on the client. For example, a younger female client may feel comfortable sitting closer to an older female solicitor but may wish to be seated further away from a male solicitor. It is helpful to have an interview environment where tables and chairs can be moved around so that the environment can be tailored to a client's needs. You could consider offering the client a choice of seating options so that they can place themselves at a comfortable physical distance from you.

2.4.5 Preparing Yourself for the Interview

Before the interview, set aside time to review whatever information you have so far received about the matter. This is likely to be limited at this point and may take the form of a few handwritten notes taken by reception staff or an initial online questionnaire completed by the client. The author recalls in their early days as a trainee, the preferred mode of communication concerning new client matters was frequently by way of coffee-stained post-it notes, with the briefest of details, something along the lines of:

> 'Mr Jones – 10am – will'

Mr Jones duly arrives for his appointment at 10am so that you can take instructions on drafting a will, and it is only natural for you to assume that this is how you are going to spend the next 45 minutes. Armed with a pen and paper, you set about taking instructions, only to discover that although Mr Jones does want a will, the more pressing matter is that he is suffering from a terminal lung disease resulting from exposure to asbestos in the workplace.

It is not uncommon to encounter a mid-interview change of direction, so you should avoid spending too much time researching what you believe to be a legal problem before meeting the client. It may turn out to be a completely different type of legal problem, or not a legal problem at all, and anyone who has spent time in a general high street firm will have experienced the 'walk- ins' or frequent visitors to the office who really just want to have a chat.

Take time before the interview to mentally prepare yourself. An initial interview is not just about the client, and it is important that you feel physically and emotionally prepared. Depending on the type of matter (and the type of client), it is an encounter that can be emotionally very demanding. As we will see in the following chapters, the solicitor is engaged the entire time using a range of skills and competencies, sometimes with difficult clients; therefore, plan your diary so that you have some time both before and after the interview to take a break, even if it is only a short one. Ensure as far as possible that the interview takes place on time. Being late for interviews can be fatal to building rapport with the client, and it puts the solicitor on the 'back foot' from the outset.

2.4.5.1 How Should You Dress for the Interview?

In section 1.10.1, we noted that the SRA requires candidates to wear clothing suitable for a business environment for the assessments and that this simply reflects what is expected in practice. Again, this may seem an obvious point to make, or maybe not. A recent LinkedIn survey by Law Firm Marketing Club on how legal professionals think they should dress revealed that a majority of professionals do not believe that dressing smartly is necessary either in Zoom meetings or in-person meetings and that "professionalism doesn't equate to what you wear".

In 2023, a London Family Law firm made headline news after it changed its dress policy. Staff were apparently sent a memo stating that they could abandon traditional office attire and dress how they liked in the spirit of self-expression. The new dress code, which permitted such items as 'electric blue sequined jackets and gold leather trousers topped with a funky pink hairdo' drew comparisons with the dress code at exclusive London private members nightclub 'Annabel's'.

Self-expression is all very well, but in legal practice, there are obviously some non-negotiables relating to attire when attending court. Legal representatives are expected to observe court dress or business attire, depending on the court. This typically involves wearing a dark-coloured suit. In addition, many firms have a dress policy which employees must adhere to, with exceptions for designated days when the firm permits employees to 'dress-down'. Even then, firms will usually have some rules about what attire is/is not acceptable.

Whether you are a fan of a pin-striped suit and bowler hat or prefer a more casual approach, it is important to remember clients' expectations. The fact is that clients expect legal professionals to dress a certain way, and this is part of the professional service offered to them. Whatever we personally feel about this, clients tend to expect their solicitor to look like the typical solicitor. Sacrificing that expectation in favour of self-expression is very risky indeed for the client/solicitor relationship. While it is, of course, true that what you wear has no bearing on the quality of the legal advice, we do need to be mindful that we present ourselves as a professional package, and how we appear to clients does matter. The safest option is to take a 'Goldilocks' approach, so not too casual as to bring into question professionalism and not so slick or extravagant that it causes a communication barrier between the solicitor and the client.

2.5 Barriers to Effective Communication

In this section, we examine the common communication barriers that can be encountered in the initial client meeting. It might be useful at this point to think about what is physically happening when we communicate verbally. In a professional setting, the encounter between a solicitor and client in a face-to-face interview involves communication in the form of an exchange of information, with both the client and the solicitor taking on the role of sender/speaker and receiver/listener of messages containing that information.

However, there is much more going on behind the scenes. Our brains use other senses to pick up visual information through non-verbal signals and sometimes even olfactory information through our sense of smell.

These different channels of communication (some of which are intentional and others not) are not happening in a vacuum. Instead, they are taking place in a particular environment (a professional one), between two people who have not met each other before. The solicitor may potentially be dealing with a client who is a first-time user of legal services and who may be anxious or vulnerable.

There might be personal factors affecting the solicitor, too, including tiredness or stress. As the success of the interview is dependent on so many factors, it is not difficult to see how a communication barrier may arise.

A communication barrier might distort information that is being exchanged or completely stop the information in its tracks. Alternatively, some information might get through to its intended destination but is misunderstood by the recipient because of the manner in which it is communicated and/or the behaviour of the recipient.

The following sections discuss some of the main communication barriers that you are likely to encounter, and some of these barriers (and the communication bridges) are expanded on in Chapters 3 and 4. It is important that you are able to recognise barriers so that you can take steps to prevent or overcome them. It is not always going to be possible to overcome every communication barrier. This would be an unrealistic expectation placed on any legal professional, but being aware of how and when they can arise is a good starting point to eliminating most of them.

There may be an obvious barrier to communication which can be easily remedied (for example, removing the pile of files preventing the client from seeing you), or perhaps you pick up clear non-verbal cues demonstrating that the client is confused or bewildered, for example, a furrowed brow or puzzled expression. Some clients may feel confident enough to indicate that there is a problem. But many will not, and it is understandable for an overwhelmed, inexperienced solicitor to miss subtle but vital signs of a communication barrier.

The other possibility is that the solicitor has a vague feeling that something is wrong but does not yet have the skills necessary to pinpoint what it is, let alone how to remedy it, with the only remaining course of action to hope for the best and plough on regardless.

The following points are not an exhaustive list of communication barriers but will hopefully serve as a starting point from which you will begin to recognise other potential barriers.

2.5.1 The Interview Room and Surrounding Areas

Physical Barriers

The most obvious obstruction to communication is the presence of a physical barrier which prevents the parties from seeing and hearing each other. The impact of not being able to see the person that you are communicating with is that non-verbal behaviours, which form part of the communication jigsaw, are missed. This is obviously more likely to be a problem when speaking to a client on the telephone or in a virtual interview; nevertheless, physical barriers can occur in a face-to-face interview in the form of poorly arranged furniture or piles of papers on the desk or table.

Noise Barriers

Whether they are on a high street in a small town or in a city centre location, the offices of law firms are usually strategically positioned to maximise footfall and commercial prominence. This can result in having to work in unavoidably noisy environments, over which a firm may have little or no direct control. However, intrusive external noise from building work will be a distraction at best and at worst, will make the interview impossible, so practical steps will have to be taken in the planning phase of the interview to minimise the effects or arrange the interview to take place in a more suitable location.

Consideration will also need to be given to clients who have hearing difficulties. Even an environment that does not appear to be affected by intrusive noise may pose a problem for clients with hearing loss. Remember that you are preparing the interview for an individual client, and there is a regulatory obligation to make reasonable adjustments.

Noise from within the offices also needs to be kept to a minimum. If clients are in an environment where they can hear the discussions of other people, then not only is it distracting, but they may also feel concerned that their private discussions can be heard by others. This will affect client/solicitor rapport and could also constitute a regulatory breach of confidentiality.

Temperature and Lighting Barriers

Take care to ensure that the temperature of the room is comfortable for the client and that you are also comfortable. Communication can be a challenge if the environment is too warm or too cold. Ask a client directly if they are warm enough/too warm and make adjustments if necessary. Likewise, if the room is too dark or too bright, this can be uncomfortable and can affect the ability to take notes. This may seem nothing other than common sense, but a study of students conducting client interviews in a legal advice centre identified that one student continued to interview a client well after darkness fell, without thinking to switch on the lights!

Remember that the needs and attributes of clients must be considered. Poor lighting is particularly problematic for those who are visually impaired, and excessive lighting can be uncomfortable and distracting.

2.5.2 Culture Gaps and Inter-Cultural Barriers

There is an abundance of literature on the impact of cultural and inter-cultural differences on communication. This guide does not attempt to unravel this complex area. Instead, we have selected some key points for you to consider:

Cultural Gaps

We can refer to cultural gaps as those that occur between individuals of essentially the same culture but different backgrounds. Even when both parties have some knowledge of each other's language, there may be misunderstandings due to differences in grammar, pronunciation, or use of vocabulary. There could also be barriers caused by the linguistic ability of a solicitor compared to that of a client. We discuss disparity in language and the use of legal jargon in more detail in section 2.6.

The fact that you are a legal professional and your client is not may cause a culture gap. You may be perceived as a member of an exclusive club, and this can create distance and barriers.

Inter-Cultural Barriers

Inter-cultural communication barriers are those that occur between people from different cultures and can be found in language (including body language), beliefs, values, and norms.

Clearly, it is going to be difficult for people who speak different languages to communicate effectively with each other without assistance, and in the planning phase of the interview, the solicitor should be sure to check if an interpreter is required. Sometimes, the client's family member or friend may want to act as an interpreter, but you should avoid this arrangement if there is a suspicion that the individual serving as the interpreter will be motivated by a personal interest in the outcome of the legal matter.

Different cultures have different body language, behaviours, and gestures that can lead to misunderstandings. Cultural norms govern how people interact with others. These norms determine factors such as punctuality, interpersonal distance, touch, use of gestures, and facial expressions.

What might be considered acceptable in one culture may be frowned upon in another. The best advice here is to know a little about your client and your client base without making assumptions. It is estimated that there are around 3,800 unique cultures in the world. We cannot know all of the cultural norms of every culture, but taking a pragmatic approach and knowing something about the culture of your clients is a good place to start.

Across cultures, differences in our cognitive patterns will be reflected in different communication styles. Western cultures apparently tend to use a linear thinking style, moving through a series of linked steps to a conclusion, whereas a circular or contextual discussion style is typical in African, Latin, Arab, and Asian cultures.

Using a different style to tell the client's story or answer a question may cause a solicitor to try and control the narrative, which could, in turn, result in a breakdown in communication between the parties.

2.5.3 The Interviewer

Barriers can arise because of the interviewer. Solicitors are as susceptible as anybody else to feeling stressed, tired, and distracted by external and internal factors, which can impact on communication. However, as professionals, we do need to develop ways of coping with both our own emotions and those of others, particularly our clients.

Not Listening and/or Not Interested

A barrier can develop if the interviewer is not listening or not listening carefully enough. The client is telling their story, but the messages are not getting through, or only some of the information is being listened to. In the preparation phase, it is important to put your own thoughts aside and clear your mind completely before beginning the process of interviewing. This can be challenging at times, but we have to learn to suspend our preoccupations temporarily.

A barrier may occur if the solicitor is simply not interested enough to listen properly. Negative body language such as fidgeting, checking a watch frequently, yawning, doodling, or sitting in a closed body position with arms crossed will demonstrate a lack of interest very clearly to a client. Avoid trying to sneak a look at a mobile phone, which should be switched off and out of sight.

Become more aware of body posture (both in the client and in yourself). Make sure your body posture is open, and your arms are not crossed. An open body posture is interpreted as being open and receptive to communication. Leaning slightly forward and establishing eye contact is a sign of attention and engagement, although be aware that in some cultures, sustained eye contact is not acceptable, so keep eye contact at an appropriate level that communicates attention but is not overbearing. A closed body posture (hunched over/arms or legs or both crossed) may be interpreted by a client as a lack of interest.

Lack of Sincerity

Insincerity can often be detected through inconsistencies between verbal and non-verbal communication, often referred to as a lack of congruence. Pretend listening, or pseudo listening, is when we display signs of listening but we are not actually listening at all, for example – 'I see, yes, absolutely!' or 'Really?' while making sympathetic noises. Clients generally pick up on pretend listening and naturally will think that the solicitor is not interested in their problem. This is likely to result in a breakdown in communication.

Lacking Essential Interviewing Skills

A solicitor may lack the essential skills needed to conduct the interview effectively. This may, for example, result in a premature narrowing down of questions or a failure to engage with active listening, which can be detrimental to communication. We will consider listening and questioning skills in more detail in Chapters 3 and 4.

Attitudes, Bias, and Stereotyping

We each develop our own biases, attitudes, values, and feelings as a result of our personal experiences in life. These factors can act as filters that warp information received and affect how we react to situations. This means that we may unconsciously judge people and be influenced by factors such as physical appearance or the way a client communicates. As the brain uses shortcuts to process familiar information, this can lead to stereotyping. A client who presents in a certain way may be stereotyped into a group, and we fail to acknowledge the full and detailed picture that relates to that particular client, instead only seeing the parts that have got through the filter. The danger is that we have already pigeon-holed the client into a pre-determined category, and so we stop listening to anything else that they have to say.

The SRA recognises the problem of stereotyping, particularly of ethnic minorities, and provides information in its resource, '*How to build trust with your client*' (31 August 2022). The SRA expects solicitors to build relationships of trust with clients from cultural or ethnic backgrounds different from one's own and makes it clear that this is a form of cultural competence. The full definition can be accessed here:

https://www.sra.org.uk/solicitors/resources/specific-areas-of-practice/building-trust-clients/

Credibility

The effectiveness of a solicitor as a communicator is partly dependent on credibility. This will be enhanced by evidence of reliability, consistency, and trustworthiness. It will be damaged by failing to respond promptly or appropriately and by inconsistent advice and decision-making.

2.5.4 The Client

Most clients are motivated to talk during an interview because their need to do so outweighs any emotional factors which might prevent them from talking. However, the reverse might also be true, and the motivation to participate in the interview may be outweighed by a client's other needs. Here are some examples:

Shame/Embarrassment

Important facts may induce feelings of embarrassment or guilt, and the client may either withhold the information or prevaricate. An example might be a client who is a victim of 'sextortion' (financially motivated sexual extortion), where criminals have threatened to release sexual or indecent images unless money is paid. The full story that the client must disclose may make the client feel acutely ashamed or embarrassed.

Trauma/Suffering

A client may avoid talking about events that are painful to recall. In many practice areas, it is the event that the client is seeking assistance with that is causing the pain. An example is a probate matter, where the client is very recently bereaved and overwhelmed by a range of emotions. Empathy will be crucial here, and a solicitor must tailor their approach to the client's needs. For example, it may be possible to encourage a client to participate once the importance of the information is explained. Alternatively, it might be necessary to postpone a meeting with a client who is too upset to communicate. Consideration also needs to be given to capacity issues for clients with severe mental health issues.

Privacy

The client's first interview with a legal professional could be described as more intimate than a physical examination by a medical professional and a sharing of sensitive information likened to a metaphorical removal of clothing for a physical examination. Some clients will simply not want to divulge deeply personal information. A solicitor needs to approach this in a non-judgmental and non-moralising way, which in turn builds trust and encourages disclosure.

2.6 Client Bridges

Bridges are strategies that we can use to overcome communication barriers. Again, it is important to understand that communication takes place in a context, and we need to understand this context to be able to build client bridges. Each client presents with a different story, background, culture, emotions, attitudes, and experiences, and all of these need to be considered to be able to overcome barriers that arise.

Listening to a client and allowing them to tell their story can be an effective communication bridge. Knowing that we are being listened to is a powerful tool for establishing trust and opening up the lines of communication. For a client who is finding it difficult to communicate, the solicitor is a trained professional who is capable, skilful, and willing to listen and help.

Careful and considerate questioning can also serve as a bridge to a client. When combined, the skills of listening and questioning can provide relief for a client from the burden of their emotions. We examine active listening and questioning together with practical strategies in more detail in Chapter 3.

As human beings, we are all, at times, motivated by self-interest. This can work to the advantage of a solicitor who is trying to encourage a client to disclose information. Pointing out to a client that disclosure of information will help to achieve the client's objective can be a very effective strategy to encourage participation. Take, for example, a personal injury claim involving injuries which have caused sexual dysfunction. A client may feel embarrassed to discuss this symptom but may be prepared to do so if they are made aware that it could increase an award of compensation.

2.7 Building Rapport

Books about skills for professionals usually include a section on the necessity of building rapport with their clients, customers, or patients, and this guide is no exception because building rapport is vitally important to the client/solicitor relationship.

Building rapport is also specifically referred to in the SQE2 interviewing assessment. The skill required of candidates is to:

Conduct Themselves in a Professional Manner and Treat the Client With Courtesy, Respect, and Politeness, Including Respecting Diversity Where Relevant

Indicators demonstrating competence are:

- The candidate behaves politely and builds rapport with the client

Indicators that do not demonstrate competence are:

- The candidate's behaviour towards the client is consistently insensitive
- The candidate has an overly familiar, casual, or highly informal manner, e.g., the candidate is flippant or makes jokes with the client
- The candidate's behaviour is rude, abrupt, dismissive, disrespectful, judgemental, or patronising

The full SQE2 Interviewing performance indicators are available here:

https://sqe.sra.org.uk/docs/default-source/pdfs/sqe2-sample-questions/int-performance-indicators.pdf?sfvrsn=69961d98_2

2.7.1 What Is 'Rapport'?

Rapport is a rather elusive concept. The word is borrowed from the French *rapporter*– to bring back.

According to the Oxford Dictionary, it means:

> a close and harmonious relationship in which groups understand each other's feelings or ideas and communicate well.

It can be obvious when it exists, and it can develop in a very short space of time. However, it is difficult at times to articulate precisely *how* it was created. Sometimes, the parties involved just seem to find that they are on the same wavelength. The bonds of trust, understanding, and confidence are formed, and the parties are more likely to exchange information and do what they can to help each other out. Some people seem to have a natural ability to create rapport, whereas others find it difficult to connect with others on this level.

Building rapport can happen gradually, over a longer period of time, but in the context of the initial client interview, it is crucial that the solicitor takes steps to build it from the moment they meet the client.

2.7.2 The Importance of Building Rapport

Building rapport is the cornerstone of the client/solicitor relationship. Failing to establish rapport will be detrimental to the client/solicitor relationship. Andrew Sherr, who has written extensively on the subject of interviewing skills, uses the analogy of medical students attending an anatomy lesson to illustrate the problem:

> It is difficult to expect doctors to see patients as real people when their whole view of medicine begins with a dead body. How do lawyers fare on this score? On the first day of legal education students are faced usually with the equivalent of a dead body. is it little wonder that lawyers see the people who bring their lives and their problems to them as 'divorce cases', 'unfair dismissals' and 'conveyancing jobs'?
>
> (A. Sherr, 1986, p. 11)

The point is that a client is a human being, not just a manifestation of a legal problem that needs to be sorted out. If you establish rapport at the first meeting, the potential client will feel relaxed enough to speak openly and will want to instruct you to handle their legal matter.

2.7.3 How Do You Build Rapport?

It is estimated that it takes as little as 10 seconds for a first impression to be made. It goes without saying that first impressions count a great deal, and it is the first few seconds of the initial meeting with a new client that will determine the direction of the relationship in terms of creating trust and confidence. Unfortunately, there is no instruction booklet on exactly how to build rapport, and the extent to which it can be built will depend on the personalities of the people involved. But, once rapport has been established, you can then continue to build on it and work to maintain it throughout the duration of the professional relationship.

Imagine that you are a client and have had your first-ever meeting with a solicitor at their offices. You have just left the offices following the conclusion of the interview, and you receive a call on your mobile telephone from a family member asking how the interview went and what the solicitor was like. What would be your own expectations of the encounter?

You would want to be able to describe the solicitor using some of the following adjectives:

- Welcoming
- Polite
- Professional
- Interested
- Knowledgeable
- Confident
- Kind
- Compassionate
- Open
- Helpful

If you are able to describe someone in any of these terms, then rapport has more than likely been established between you.

Now read the following extract describing an encounter when rapport has not been established:

> I feel a bit upset, to be honest. He was 30 minutes late and seemed in a rush. He was finishing his lunch and didn't even look up when I came in. He took my name and a few details and didn't seem very interested. It felt as though I was talking to myself! He didn't listen to anything I said. I was trying to tell him what happened that night, but he kept interrupting and asking questions I didn't know anything about. When I got out of that office, I burst into tears!

While people who are good at building rapport are unable to say why they are good at it, people who struggle to build it are able to articulate that it is often because they do not know how to break the ice with a new person, in other words, they find small talk challenging and fear coming across as insincere.

Here are some tips to help establish rapport at the first meeting: You may think some of these are just common sense and do not need to be reinforced here, but in the highly pressured environment of legal practice, common sense can sometimes make itself rather scarce!

The first and most immensely important tip is to be on time for the interview. Delays can increase client anxiety and can be fatal to building rapport. Of course, delays are occasionally unavoidable, in which case, clients should be kept informed by reception, wherever possible.

A warm and friendly welcome and introduction will ease a client's nerves. Greet the client with a smile and make eye contact. A smile (the right kind of smile for the right situation) will make you approachable from the moment you meet the client. Be aware of cultural differences in greetings. For example, shaking hands may be seen as a sign of respect in the Western world, but it may not be appropriate in some cultures.

If the client is brought by a member of staff to the office or conference room where you are seated, stand up and go over to greet them at the door. If the client is introduced by a member of staff, say, "Hello, Mr/Mrs/Miss", and say that you are pleased to meet them. Introduce yourself. If you are collecting the client from reception, go up to the client and address them by name, then introduce yourself.

Many people find a first meeting with strangers awkward and embarrassing. This may be due to nerves about the reason for the meeting or simply a degree of shyness when starting a conversation with strangers. Inexperienced solicitors may lack the confidence to take the first step in a professional introduction. It need not be an intimidating experience for either party involved in the interview. Having a plan of how you will greet new clients is a useful way of taking some of the apprehension out of the situation, and if you have taken time to prepare for the interview, this will help to build confidence.

In general, people seek the assistance of a solicitor when they are worried about a legal issue. One might think that client anxiety would be confined to certain types of legal work, for example, contentious family or criminal proceedings, but even a straightforward transaction such as a house purchase can cause clients to feel stressed. However nervous you may be feeling, remember that the client is likely to be feeling this even more so. Greeting the client properly will extinguish many of those uncomfortable feelings for both parties.

You might say, "Hello, I'm Steph Brown. You must be Mr Bowden", or, "Hello, Mr Bowden, I'm Steph Brown". Using your own first and last name is probably the right balance. Law Society guidance on client care at the initial interview also states that when a client attends an interview, you should explain to them your status within the firm, i.e., trainee solicitor, legal executive, solicitor, etc.

Basic acts of kindness and concern go a long way in building rapport. If a client seems flustered, bewildered, or agitated, ask them if they are okay and give them a moment to get used to the surroundings. Offer to take coats and bags, ask if they have been offered something to drink by reception, or ask if they want anything. Steer the client towards chairs but then let the client choose which chair (if there is a choice).

Break the ice with some small talk, for example, "How was your journey/have you travelled far?" or, "How was the parking/traffic?" Small talk should be about the client, not you. If you ask these types of icebreaker questions with sincerity, it will not feel superficial, but if you are simply box-ticking, this will be obvious to the client. The key is not to overthink an icebreaker and to approach it as the informal part of the interview process, the purpose of which is to help the client (and you) relax. If you are friendly and approachable, most clients will mirror your behaviour and will relax during the interview. A caveat is that if a client is visibly upset or very agitated, re-assess whether small talk is appropriate at all.

Once seated, it is a good idea to ask the client to confirm their full name if you do not already know it. Remember also that clients may forget your name (probably very shortly after the introduction), so having a business card (old fashioned but effective) to give to the client at the beginning of the interview is a good idea. They then have this to refer to during the interview if they forget your name.

You should explain what your role is within the firm, if you will be handling the case, and who your supervisor is, if you have one, and explain that they will be supervising the matter. A problem that can arise here is that more junior legal professionals may feel awkward at having to explain that they are junior, as they may feel that the client will not have full confidence in them. It is, however, best to explain your role at the outset.

2.7.4 How Do You Rebuild Rapport?

Rapport can be lost for many reasons, including poor listening and questioning skills, insincerity, and lack of empathy. This can lead to a loss of trust and confidence on the part of the client. It is possible for rapport to be re-established and for trust and confidence to be salvaged. Again, this may be self-evident, but whether the cause is lateness or poor communication, or you have made a mistake, if your actions are the cause of the loss of rapport, the error should be acknowledged, and a genuine apology should be forthcoming. This is usually sufficient to re-establish rapport.

It may be the case that the relationship is not salvageable. Unfortunately, some clients have unrealistic expectations of the client/solicitor relationship, and this can take its toll on a solicitor's time and emotional reserves. In circumstances where a client persistently and unreasonably challenges aspects of a solicitor's practice and attempts to re-establish rapport have failed, it may be necessary to consider termination of the retainer.

2.8 Balancing Empathy

> I only wish I could have found another solicitor because I honestly thought she just didn't give a damn, couldn't care less, as though it's an everyday thing. It probably is for her, but this is the first time I've gone through this. I mean, I didn't think that I was special, but I just wanted a little bit of – not sympathy exactly, I didn't want the solicitor to feel sorry for me – just concern, I think, to understand what I was going through and that I wasn't going completely mad! I was going to them for help. I just ended up feeling really stupid for going, and I don't think I'm going to win my case.

Reading this statement, what do you think was the client's main complaint about her solicitor? Here, the client's feelings about the lack of concern of the solicitor can be translated into wider fears about the whole service she is receiving. You need to think about how you can prevent such a situation from arising. Your ability to relate to clients on a personal level is vital in keeping the lines of communication open and in nurturing the professional relationship. A very important characteristic in this context is the idea of empathy.

Empathy is a difficult notion to pin down and is often confused with other feelings, such as compassion and sympathy. However, to be an empathetic legal practitioner, empathy must be distinguished from compassion and sympathy.

Sympathy is when we feel pity or sorrow for the misfortune of others. For example, I may sympathise with the plight of victims of an earthquake, but I also feel a sense of relief about *not* experiencing what those victims are experiencing. Sympathy can create emotional distance between people, although it can, of course, trigger a response of a need to help in some way, and this can be described as compassion. Compassion can be described as the emotional response to sympathy or empathy which motivates us to help others.

It could be argued that empathy is not really an emotion at all, but instead, it can be regarded an ability to assess what is being experienced internally by someone else.

Empathy, then, is being able to tap into the emotions and feelings that another person is experiencing, and it is a vital component in a client-centred approach. Empathy is only possible if the client is treated as a human being rather than simply a legal problem that needs to be solved, and a failure to demonstrate genuine empathy can result in damage to the client/solicitor relationship. What is needed then is not only thinking about the legal problem/how to resolve it but also understanding how the client perceives their legal problem and how it impacts them personally.

Some solicitors, particularly those new to legal practice, may feel uneasy focusing on emotions, preferring instead the safety of books and legal principles. Indeed, some legal professionals may have chosen law as a career in the mistaken hope of avoiding having to deal with emotions. However, being empathetic does not mean sinking so deep into someone else's problems that they become an emotional burden on you. Instead, being empathetic involves taking a step back and setting aside any preconceived ideas and prejudices so that you can understand a client's perspective. It really is the glue that holds the relationship together, and if a client feels that a solicitor lacks genuine empathy, they may feel a lack of confidence about how the legal matter will be handled.

Within the context of the initial client interview, empathy begins with taking time to *really* listen to a client. Through active listening, a solicitor can reinforce a client's feelings of trust and confidence, which in turn facilitates more effective communication (as well as reducing client anxieties). The reason for this is that humans by their nature have a fundamental need to be listened to, understood, and, most importantly, not judged. We will consider active listening in more detail in Chapter 3.

An empathetic interviewer also carefully utilises questioning techniques, for example, mirroring, which we will discuss in Chapter 4. Finally, empathy is crucial in the advising phase of the interview, where we should take a holistic approach to the client's goals and needs. We consider advice in more detail in Chapter 5.

Here are some ideas to help you with empathy:

- Give the client the courtesy of your full attention and avoid multitasking during the interview (put away mobile phones and laptops).
- While the client is talking, listen actively and try to avoid thinking about what you will say next.
- Pay close attention to the client's non-verbal messages through their body language and voice.
- Reflect back to the client your understanding of their feelings and emotions.
- Acknowledge how the client's legal problem makes them feel.
- Avoid legal jargon and long, complex sentences.
- Pause between paragraphs to give clients time to process your explanations and their own emotions.

2.9 Equality in Language – The Pitfalls of Sounding Like a Lawyer

Communication problems can often arise because a solicitor is using technical legal language which the client does not understand. Conversely, communication issues can also occur because of a client's misuse of terms or ambiguous expressions, which the solicitor does not understand. Clients must be in a position to make informed decisions based on information received but this is not going to be possible if the parties are talking at cross purposes.

Appropriate use of language is recognised within the SQE2 interviewing assessment, and the requirement is to:

> Communicate and explain in a way that is suitable for the client to understand.

Indicators that demonstrate competence are:

- The candidate uses language which is easily understood by the client.
- Where it is necessary to use technical language that a client would not understand, the candidate explains the legal terms clearly and succinctly (e.g., 'restrictive covenant'; 'legal easement'; 'age contingency'; 'nil rate band').

Indicators that do not demonstrate competence are:

- The candidate's explanations are verbose, legalistic, complicated, rambling, or confused and not understood by the client.
- The candidate uses technical language when necessary but provides little, if any, explanation, and/or the explanations provided are vague, even when questioned by the client.

You can access the full performance indicators for the client SQE2 interview assessment here:

https://sqe.sra.org.uk/docs/default-source/pdfs/sqe2-sample-questions/int-performance-indicators.pdf?sfvrsn=69961d98_2

Legal English is a unique mixture of Anglo-Saxon vocabulary and words that have their origins in other cultures and languages, for example, Latin (*caveat emptor, ab initio, novus actus interveniens, ad hoc, de facto, bona fide, inter alia*, and *ultra vires*, to name a few!), French (*abus de droit*, chattel, lease, executor) and even Old Norse (trust). Legal English is the result of historical, political, and social developments going back many centuries (Schneiderova, 2018).

Just to confuse matters further, there are also words commonly used in the English language which have different meanings when used in a legal context. Within the legal world, this shared legal language can foster a sense of unity and belonging, but for lay people, it baffles and confuses. When we enter legal practice, the terminology we have spent so long learning must then be converted back to language that lay clients can understand.

In 1971, frustrated with the jargon used by Liverpool City Council to explain the benefits system, a semi-literate woman from Liverpool set out to 'wipe out gobbledygook and legalese'. This marked the beginning of the Plain English Campaign (www.plainenglish.co.uk). In 1983, the Law Society Gazette published a letter from a surveyor complaining about legalese in leases. This prompted a solicitor working in local government to invite readers to form an organisation (Clarity) to promote the use of plain language in the legal professions. The project was even endorsed by Lord Denning, and Clarity now has members in over 650 countries. An example can be seen in The Civil Procedure Rules 1998, which introduced the term 'claimant' to replace the archaic term 'plaintiff'. You can access further information about Clarity here: www.clarity-international.org.

While the primary aim of the Plain English Campaign and Clarity appears to apply to the written word, legal professionals must also ensure that plain English is used in oral communication, including interviews. This is a key interaction between the client and the solicitor, and it is crucial that matters are explained in a straightforward and accessible way.

As we have seen in the section earlier in this chapter, CCS 3.4 requires solicitors to take account of clients' attributes, needs, and circumstances when providing legal services. The SRA is particularly concerned with ensuring that solicitors adapt their services to enable vulnerable people to access them fully.

In addition, CCS 8.6 requires that solicitors give clients information in a way they can understand so that they are "in a position to make informed decisions about the services they need, how their matter will be handled and the options available to them".

This is achieved by breaking down principles and concepts into simple vocabulary that is easy to understand and using it in short, straightforward sentences. Using an analogy or an example can be a useful tool; for example, elements of negligence can be explained as ingredients in a recipe or hurdles in a race. Visual aids such as diagrams and flowcharts can also provide helpful scaffolding to make technical language easier for clients to understand.

Solicitors must be able to switch between legal and everyday language. This is a form of translation. For example, many non-lawyers may not be aware of the forms of property ownership and the distinction between a joint tenancy and tenancy in common. If you are instructed by a client to prepare a will which includes provision for property, and the client tells you that they own the property jointly, you will need to know whether this is held as tenants in common or as joint tenants. The first stage of the translation process is to explain the difference to the client in plain English and find out the joint ownership position. Then, if it is a joint tenancy, you will have to move to the next stage of the translation, which is to explain that it will need to be transferred into a tenancy in common so that the share of the property can be disposed in the will.

Same Words – Different Meaning

A common problem is that the same word can have different meanings to different people. Non-lawyers may use words in the wrong context and refer to concepts such as 'breach of contract' and 'negligence' without realising the meaning in a legal sense.

Read the following example, which concerns a complaint to the Legal Ombudsman:

> Mr G wrote to his solicitor complaining that they had acted negligently by not keeping him informed of the progress of his personal injury claim and by not responding to his emails or letters. In his letter, Mr G alleged that the firm had been negligent. The firm told him that he needed to draft a pre-action protocol compliant letter of claim so that they could forward it to their insurers. Mr G informed the firm that he did not intend to make a negligence claim, but they insisted he provide them with a letter of claim.
>
> Mr G referred his complaint to the Legal Ombudsman, and, at that point, the firm asked for an opportunity to deal with it under their internal complaints process. Their request was refused as they had already had this opportunity and had decided not to deal with the complaint. Following an investigation, the Legal Ombudsman found that the firm had progressed Mr G's case, and they had kept him reasonably informed. However, the firm had not dealt with Mr G's complaint properly. It was clear from Mr G's complaint letter that the complaint related to service rather than negligence. The firm was ordered to pay Mr G compensation of £150 for the distress caused to him in the way they handled the matter.

In summary

- Ensure you comply with the SRA Standards and Regulation and statutory obligations of equality, diversity, and inclusion.
- Show a commitment to ethical behaviour and conduct at all times, including during the initial client interview, and avoid unethical behaviour that could result in disciplinary proceedings.
- Recognise the ethics and professional conduct issues which may occur in an interviewing context and ensure you are able to identify when an ethical or professional conduct issue arises.
- Act in the best interest of each client and satisfy yourself that, when taking initial instructions, you are meeting the needs of vulnerable clients and taking into account an individual's attributes, needs, and circumstances.
- As an SQE candidate, demonstrate the ability to act in accordance with the SRA Standards and Regulations and ensure you know how to answer questions on ethics and professional conduct, which are assessed pervasively.
- Familiarise yourself with the underlying principles of legal interviewing and appreciate its importance in the role of the solicitor, particularly the initial client interview.
- Understand the aims and objectives of the initial client interview from your own perspective and from the perspective of a client.

- Know what skills and competencies are required to conduct an effective interview and consider the structure of an initial client interview.
- Recognise that being a client-centred legal professional is crucial in building a relationship of trust and confidence.
- Ensure that all practical steps that are within your control have been taken to create the right atmosphere, including choosing the interview location, preparing the interview room, and preparing yourself.
- Consider barriers to communication which can arise and how to build client bridges.
- Understand the importance of building rapport from the moment you meet a client and know techniques that can be used to help build and rebuild rapport.
- Recognise the importance of empathy within the client/solicitor relationship. Appreciate the difference between empathy and other concepts, for example, sympathy and compassion, and recognise that empathy must be balanced.
- Ensure that you are using language in a way that a client understands and which takes into account a client's individual attributes, needs, and circumstances.

Key Practice Case

Solicitors Disciplinary Tribunal Decision: Vulnerable clients

The following anonymised case was referred by the SRA to the SDT. It concerned a solicitor who failed to identify signs of fraud and exploitation of a vulnerable client.

Mr G was a solicitor with over 30 years of experience in conveyancing. He was acting on behalf of the buyer and the seller in a property matter, which raised the risk of a conflict of interest in the transaction. Client X was autistic and had an estimated mental age of 12. Mr G had significant concerns about Client X's mental capacity and doubted whether he was able to manage his own financial affairs, including entering into contracts. Client X was a vulnerable individual.

The buyer of the property was a company owned by Client Y. Mr G had a long-standing professional relationship with Client Y. Mr G continued to act in the transfer of the property from Client X to Client Y. despite there being no payment or formal agreement allowing Client X to continue to live in the property. In the client care letter to Client X, Mr G failed to advise on whether the transaction was sensible or reasonable.

In addition, Mr G failed to:

- Make enquiries in relation to the transaction
- Meet the client on their own to advise of the risks

- Determine whether the transfer was in the client's best interests
- Take steps to protect the client's interests, including any right they had to continue to live on the property

Mr G failed to make enquiries on Client X's behalf that would have revealed that he had been convicted of fraud and money laundering, receiving a custodial sentence of over five years.

The case was referred by the SRA to the SDT. The SDT found that Mr G had breached five SRA Principles from the SRA Code of Conduct 2011, including failing to act with integrity and independence, failing to act in the best interests of Client X, and failing to protect Client X's money.

The SDT was also very concerned that the solicitor had previously been fined in relation to five conveyancing matters in which they acted without instructions, failed to carry out necessary due diligence, and did not register lenders' charges.

The solicitor agreed an order for costs of £12,000 and was suspended for 12 months.

Practice Tips

- Before you begin interviewing, take time to ensure that you have a sound understanding of the relevant ethical and professional conduct rules set by the SRA, as well as the regulatory framework within which the rules operate.
- If you are unsure about any aspect of ethical and professional conduct, seek help from a senior colleague, refer to guidance from the SRA, or contact their Professional Ethics helpline for support.
- Remember that CCS 3.4 and CCF 4.2 require you to consider and take account of your client's attributes, needs, and circumstances. Before an interview, make sure that you know if the client has any particular requirements that need to be taken into account in the planning stage and make necessary adjustments.
- Consider whether you need an interpreter and book in advance.
- Ensure that within your schedule, you set aside some time before the interview to prepare yourself.
- Organise your diary (or ask those responsible for making appointments) so that meetings and interviews are timed with sufficient intervals between them to avoid overrunning (and being late).
- Prepare the interview room in advance. Set the stage for an effective interview by paying attention to how best to obtain information from the client by providing an environment that is safe, comfortable, and in line with client-centred principles.

- Greet the client appropriately and in a warm and friendly manner so that you can immediately build rapport, confidence, and trust.
- Confirm your name and status within the firm.
- You will still come across to the client as a professional while being relaxed with a client.
- Appearance matters, and first impressions are vitally important so ensure that you are dressed appropriately for the client interview.

Practice Risks

- Failing to know and understand the professional rules and codes of conduct relevant to interviewing.
- Failing to seek guidance and support from senior colleagues and/or the SRA on matters relating to ethical and professional conduct.
- Neglecting to consider the client's individual attributes, needs, and circumstances leads to difficulties in establishing the client/solicitor relationship.
- Failing to consider the importance of interview planning and preparation.
- Neglecting to consider your own needs in the preparation and planning phase of the interview. You have a pivotal role in the interview.
- Not dressing appropriately for an interview. This could create the wrong impression and affect the client/solicitor relationship.

Exercises

EXERCISE A

Pablo is a solicitor specialising in private client matters, including property and wills administration.

Lydia is an elderly widow who has recently suffered a stroke. She has made an appointment to see Pablo at his offices. She wants her son Jack to come to the appointment with her. The receptionist takes some brief details to pass to Pablo as follows:

> Lydia has decided to move in with Jack and his family and wants to sell her house. Jack has been looking after her since the stroke, and she wants to help him financially as he has been really struggling since he lost his job. Lydia would like Pablo to deal with the house sale, but she also wishes to make some changes to her will because it currently leaves everything to Jack and Jill, her daughter, in equal shares, but she does not want to leave Jill anything now. They fell out after a huge argument, and Jill is now estranged from the family.

What ethical and professional conduct issues must Pablo consider?

EXERCISE B

Test your Knowledge – Multiple Choice Tests

Test 1

A Private Client law firm which is regulated by the SRA has recently recruited two legal assistants into its domestic property department. The legal assistants will be assisting a team of solicitors with their case files.
Which one of the following statements most accurately represents the regulatory obligations that apply to the new legal assistants?

A. There are no specific regulatory obligations that apply to the legal assistants because they are not qualified solicitors.
B. As employees of an SRA-regulated firm, the legal assistants are subject to the Code of Conduct for Solicitors.
C. As employees of an SRA-regulated firm, the legal assistants are subject to the Code of Conduct for Firms.
D. As employees of an SRA-regulated firm, the legal assistants are subject to the Code of Conduct for Solicitors and the Code of Conduct for Firms.
E. The legal assistants must ensure they are aware of the provisions within the Code of Conduct for Solicitors because, as part of their role, they may carry out the tasks of a solicitor.

Test 2

A newly qualified solicitor in the Wills and Probate department of a firm has been asked by a senior partner to interview a new client who wishes to make a will.

Which one of the following statements most accurately describes how the newly qualified solicitor should not conduct the interview?

A. Set out all the options available to the client once enough information has been obtained from the client.
B. Explain legal terminology and issues using clear and concise language.
C. Make sure that the legal explanations given fit the client's circumstances.
D. Make sure that the client is treated as an individual rather than a legal problem.
E. Provide the client with technical legal explanations wherever possible.

Self-Reflection Checklist

What three important things have you learnt from this chapter?	**1**	**2**	**3**
Set out the three additional steps that you need to take to learn the skills in this chapter in more detail.	**1**	**2**	**3**

References

Books

Sherr A, *Client Interviewing for Lawyers* (Sweet and Maxwell 1986).

Tolkien JRR, *The Hobbit* (Harper Collins 1993).

Journal Article

Schneiderova A, 'Historical Background to English Legal Language' [2018] Journal of Modern Science 117–26.

Legislation

Care Act 2014

Equality Act 2010

Legal Services Act 2007

Solicitors Act 1974

Reports

LexisNexis Bellwether Report 2015 Issue 3: The Age of the Client

Websites

www.clarity-international.org

www.legalombudsman.org.uk

www.thelegalservicesboard.org.uk

www.plainenglish.co.uk

www.solicitorstribunal.org.uk

www.sra.org.uk

www.step.org

www.lawsociety.org.uk

3 Listening Skills

Key Chapter Points

1. The role of listening is recognised within legal practice and SQE2 as a core skill in oral communication.
2. Listening is different to hearing as it involves psychological input, which takes effort.
3. Interviewers need to have effective listening skills to elicit accurate and relevant information.
4. Developing the skills of listening leads to better communication, rapport and trust between the client and solicitor.
5. Listening is not purely intuitive; it is a skill that can be developed and learned.
6. Listening techniques can be used to maximise client engagement.
7. Passive listening is key to helping a client open up and tell their story during the interview process.
8. Active listening includes listening for emotions and messages sent via non-verbal communication, as these may contain important information.

3.1 Introduction

The ability to listen and question effectively is clearly fundamental to effective communication in any context, and it is widely recognised that poor listening skills are a barrier to effective communication in both our personal and professional lives. Evidence shows that this can lead to problems in relationships, health, and competency in the workplace. Of the four forms of communication (listening, speaking, reading, and writing), it is listening that we are engaged in most frequently (Kline, 1996), and we are engaged more frequently in listening in the workplace compared to in our personal lives (Hargie & Dickson, 2005).

Listening is a vital skill in the client interview process, and the ability to listen effectively to a client is a key factor in the eventual, successful outcome of the legal matter, the establishment and maintenance of the client/solicitor relationship, and overall client satisfaction with the service received.

DOI: 10.4324/9781003519096-3

This chapter will take you through the essentials of how to listen professionally and purposefully within an interview setting so that you can build rapport with the client, begin to gather the information that is needed and gain insight into the client's situation. We begin by considering how listening skills are assessed in SQE2, and then we will examine what listening is, its importance in the initial client interview, techniques for effective listening, and how to use them in initial client interviews.

3.2 Listening Skills in SQE2

The importance of listening skills is recognised in the SQE2 interviewing assessment, and candidates are expected to:

> Listen to the client and use questioning effectively to enable the client to tell the solicitor what is important to them.

The indicators demonstrating competence are:

- The candidate demonstrates active listening skills and engagement with the client, for example by
    - Listening attentively (use of facial expressions/body language/tone of voice/may evidence this),
    - Avoiding interrupting the client,
    - Listening without judgement, and
    - Avoiding making assumptions.

The indicators that do not demonstrate competence are:

- The candidate appears disinterested (e.g., facial expressions/body language/tone of voice indicate a lack of engagement with the client).
- The candidate appears distracted/reluctant to address the client's concerns (e.g., tied to their own agenda/over-reliant on their notes/repeating information the client has already provided/interrupting the client).

You can access the full performance indicators for the client SQE2 interview assessment here:

https://sqe.sra.org.uk/docs/default-source/pdfs/sqe2-sample-questions/int-performance-indicators.pdf?sfvrsn=69961d98_2

3.3 Listening or Hearing?

Before proceeding any further, let us clear up any confusion about what is meant by listening and hearing. Although often used interchangeably, they are very different activities. While 'hearing' is an involuntary and physiological perception of sound, 'listening' is a voluntary, psychological process. This means that it takes effort. We probably would not associate listening with a huge degree of effort, and this is perhaps true in many of our day-to-day activities, where listening is happening more or less spontaneously, and the stakes are low. However, the more challenging the listening task, the harder our cognitive abilities must work to successfully understand what we are listening to. There is a growing interest in the correlation between listening effort and listening fatigue, or compassion fatigue, which is a recognised symptom experienced by professional listeners such as counsellors.

Hearing happens unconsciously as sound waves reach our ears, but listening involves a conscious effort by the brain to make sense of the sounds that we are hearing. At the same time, the brain is also processing non-verbal messages in the form of body language. As it is a conscious activity, it is possible to learn, practice, and develop it, and there has been research that shows that those who are trying hard to listen demonstrate physical signs which can be picked up as increased brain effort on EEG scans.

Hearing is, of course, the first stage in the process of communication, and through the perception of sound using our ears, it enables us able to navigate the world around us. However, the stages of listening that follow help us to form vital social bonds and make meaning of the world.

There is also confusion around some of the terminology used to describe forms of listening, particularly the meaning of 'passive listening' and 'active listening'. You might also come across terms such as responsive, empathetic, and expressive listening, which are other forms of active listening. The easiest way to think about it is that 'listening' can happen on different levels, ranging from not listening at all (ignoring or pretending to listen) to more active techniques which involve a deep level of understanding. Listening techniques can often be distinguished from each other depending on the level of involvement of the listener.

3.4 Listening and Non-Verbal Communication

There are other important facets of listening which we might not ordinarily associate with listening but which should not be overlooked. We need to also 'listen' for messages sent through non-verbal communication. If we fail to listen to non-verbal communication, we will not understand the full meaning of the verbal message.

Most face-to-face communication is actually of the non-verbal variety. When we are speaking, it is almost impossible not to use non-verbal communication. Even sitting perfectly still, with eyes closed, will send a message to others – maybe something along the lines of "leave me alone!" or "I wish I was somewhere else!"

Non-verbal communication is multi-channelled and takes the form of both auditory and visual messages. It can even include olfactory messages detected by our sense of smell. For example, a smelly child with unwashed clothing can sometimes trigger alarm bells regarding potential abuse, neglect, or poverty. In the same way, a client presenting with very poor hygiene could be living in poverty or suffering from a mental or physical health issue. The different forms of non-verbal communication are important in an interview because being an effective listener also means being able to read messages, feelings, and emotions accompanying the verbal information.

3.4.1 Auditory Messages – Paralanguage (Prosody)

Paralanguage or prosody refers to non-word sounds that supplement verbal messages and provide another layer of meaning. It is the non-verbal or non-lexical vocalisations we all use to express ourselves. Examples are sighs, grunts, snorts, or expressions such as "um, hmm, urgh!" Other more subtle modifications, such as changes in pitch, stress, and intonation, or rhythm, tone, inflection, and patterns of pauses in speech are also aspects of paralanguage.

3.4.2 Visual Messages – Body Language

In Chapter 2, we considered how a solicitor's body language can act as a barrier to communication. Here, we focus our attention on the body language of a client, which a solicitor must 'listen' to. During any form of interpersonal communication, the parties involved are consciously and unconsciously using body language to provide information. Whole books have been dedicated to the subject, and one that we can recommend is *The Definitive Book of Body Language* by Allan and Barbara Pease. Read it if you have time, as it is fascinating and inciteful. In their book, they describe an experiment with tourists at a tourist information office. Here is the gist of the experiment:

> The tourists asked for information about local sightseeing attractions and were directed to a counter where they spoke to a tourism officer, who was a blond male with a moustache wearing a shirt and tie. After a few minutes, he bent down to get some brochures, and another male, clean-shaven with dark hair and wearing a blue shirt, appeared from under the counter with the brochures and continued where the blond tourist officer had left off. Around half the tourists failed to notice the change. Men were twice as likely as women to miss the swap completely!

The conclusion drawn from the experiment is that some people have very poor observational skills. However, as a solicitor, these skills need to be developed so that we do not miss vital body language information.

It is not possible to provide a full list of all body language in this guide, as it is estimated that there are over one million non-verbal cues. But we are probably all familiar with some of the more common and universal body movements and expressions, for example:

- Folded arms and legs demonstrating defensiveness or fear
- Smiling demonstrating happiness
- Nodding the head indicating 'yes'
- Shaking the head from side to side to indicate 'no'
- Hands in pockets demonstrating reluctance to talk

The topic of body language is studied as a social science in its own right and even has its own academic journal (*Journal of Nonverbal Behavior*). However, it is an area in which the main principles remain heavily disputed by experts in the field. It may turn out to be an unreliable source of information because the meaning of body language is very much dependent on context and must be examined as part of the whole communication process, including all verbal and non-verbal messages. For example, you may interpret that a client who is hunched over with arms folded and head turned downwards is disengaged or hostile when, in fact, they are just cold!

There are also cultural differences in body language we need to bear in mind, examples being the use of eye contact and shaking hands as a greeting. Cultures differ in terms of the meaning that is attributed to silence in an interaction, the degree of formality that is expected, the appropriateness of interruptions, the meaning of eye contact, and the extent of personal space.

In an interview, we need to keep a careful lookout for body language which we think is telling us something important, while appreciating that the signs we are observing may not be conclusive of anything significant when examined in context.

We also need to be careful that we are reading body language in clusters to be able to understand the underlying message. A cluster is the equivalent of a sentence and is made up of at least three gestures.

Read the following example and think about what the cluster of body language might suggest.

> Legs tightly crossed and one arm across chest with middle finger covering the mouth, thumb supporting the chin and index finger pointing upwards.
>
> (Pease & Pease, 2016)

It is also important to make sure that your own body language does not become a possible barrier to communication. It means, as a minimum, that you need to increase your own awareness of the kinds of signals you are sending to a client.

3.4.3 Visual Messages – Appearance

> Though the boots which she was wearing were not unlike each other, they were really odd ones; the one having a slightly decorated toe-cap, and the other a plain one. One was buttoned only in the two lower buttons out of five, and the other at the first, third and fifth. Now, when you see that a young lady, otherwise neatly dressed, has come away from home with odd boots, half-buttoned, it is no great deduction to say that she came away in a hurry.
>
> (Arthur Conan Doyle, 2011)

This quote from *A Case of Identity* by Arthur Conan Doyle illustrates the importance of observing a client's appearance alongside other non-verbal messages. We saw in Chapter 2 that the appearance of the solicitor is important to clients. The appearance of a client can also be important because it may contain information which supplements or contradicts the verbal and/or other non-verbal messages being sent by the client.

3.5 The Lost Art of Listening

Generally, legal professionals think that they possess excellent listening skills, but research suggests otherwise. As was mentioned in Chapter 1, the 2015 LexisNexis Bellwether Report documents the discrepancy between how good solicitors think they are at listening and what clients think. The findings were concerning. This research highlights a wider problem, which is that we generally believe we are better listeners than we are. Specifically, with reference to solicitors, this presents a dual problem. Firstly, there is an inability to listen effectively and secondly, there is a failure to reflect critically on the lack of skills.

This fits with a global concern relating to listening skills. In her book *You're Not Listening*, journalist Kate Murphy describes what she refers to as the 'lost art' of listening in modern life and the resulting loneliness, isolation, and depression that can be experienced.

> If we pause for a moment and think about how, in recent years, we have been motivated to view ourselves and our position in the world, there has been a profound shift to a more self absorbed approach. There is an excessive focus on leading conversations, being heard at all times and shouting the loudest to get our point across. What we have lost touch with is how to be quiet and how to connect with others by listening considerately and effectively.

We can reflect on effective listening by thinking about how it feels not to be listened to. The speaker quickly loses confidence and may feel that they cannot talk openly to the person not listening.

3.6 The Essentials of Professional Listening

If you take a few minutes to think about the listening activities that you engage with on a typical day, you discover that there is a mixture of what can be classed as 'voluntary' or accidental listening activities and those that we might classify as 'compulsory' listening activities. In other words, there are some activities that we do because we want to, and there are those that we do because we must do them as part of our responsibilities.

When we are talking to a friend, no one is forcing us to listen. Indeed, the friend may not be aware that while they are talking to us, we have been daydreaming about our next holiday or what to have for dinner. There may be times when we stop listening halfway through a dull conversation only to switch back in when our interest is piqued by some tantalising piece of information. During the time we have switched off, we are still hearing, but we have temporarily stopped listening.

In our professional lives, there is an expectation that we will be fully engaged in the process of listening. In some professions and industries, listening is particularly high stakes. A pilot cannot switch in and out of listening to instructions from ground control without risking the lives of passengers, and similarly, health professionals responsible for prescribing drugs need to be sure they have listened effectively so as not to make a fatal mistake.

Professional listening in the context of a client interview has certain key functions. We are trying to:

- Encourage disclosure from the client of all relevant information
- Understand the information
- Understand the client's goals and needs
- Show interest and concern for the client

In professional listening, we need to make a commitment to paying attention and maintaining it at a proficient level throughout the entirety of the professional encounter. We cannot zone in and out when we are listening in a professional capacity as this is likely to result in a loss of important information and client trust, and we may not get another opportunity to obtain the lost information or regain trust.

Professional listening in the context of the initial client interview includes passive and active listening techniques, which are explained in the following sections.

3.7 Passive Listening

Passive listening refers to techniques used to help clients open up but with very little input from the solicitor. The objective is to get a client talking and for them to state the problem as they see it. It is mostly one-way communication, which involves patience and concentration on the part of the listener. The following sections examine some of the approaches that can be utilised.

3.7.1 Start With an Open Question

It may seem strange to include a section on questioning in a chapter dedicated to listening, but the interview has to be started off, and it is the solicitor's job to do this by asking the first question. We look in detail at questioning techniques, including open questions, in Chapter 4, but a brief explanation is provided here.

An open question is one which does not try to elicit specific information. It is an invitation to a client to talk freely and enables the solicitor to begin the process of collecting information.

The open questions that you use will very much depend on what you already know about the client's matter, but some examples of open questions to start off the interview are:

- How can I help you today?
- Could you start by telling me what happened?
- Tell me about that day.
- Can you tell me about . . . ?
- Can you start by giving me some background information?

As solicitors, we should anticipate that clients may feel anxious about attending an interview. People instruct solicitors because they have a legal problem which they are unable to resolve on their own, and it can be enormously stressful dealing with the combined effects of a legal matter and an appointment with a solicitor. Clients need to talk and be understood, and this can be hugely cathartic. You will need to think carefully about how to open up the interview so that the client engages in the process.

3.7.2 Silence Is Golden

Silence in a conversation can sometimes be awkward; however, in the framework of an interview with a new client, it can be a useful technique to draw out the client's story. After asking an initial, open question, inexperienced interviewers who are new to this comparatively passive part of the process may be tempted to step in after only a few seconds and fill the silence by asking a more restrictive, closed question in the belief that this will be helpful to a client and will motivate them to speak. This may be well-intentioned but will most probably derail the client's thought process and elicit a narrower or incomplete range of information. Clients should be given sufficient time and space to gather their thoughts together and formulate a response, particularly if the issues are sensitive or challenging to recall and vocalise.

It can be really difficult to hold back from trying to make order of a jumbled collection of facts and recollections, and with time pressures, we think that we will save time by jumping in and directing the narrative. This should be avoided as an uninterrupted story will, in the long run, be more time efficient and will prevent loss of important information.

Think about an occasion when you have told *your* story to a listener. Maybe this was in response to a simple question, for example, how was your holiday/weekend/evening? If you are constantly being steered in a direction the listener wants to go in, do you go willingly? You will probably find that you try to hook up where you left off (before the interruption), or you get confused and end up missing out information.

Silence can be problematic when it is not suggestive of a client simply needing more time to respond. It may instead be an indication that a client does not want to talk. A prolonged period of silence in these circumstances is not going to be helpful as it will make the client feel uncomfortable, which in turn could affect trust and confidence. The skill is knowing when to let a silence continue and when to end it and rescue a client by stepping in. Here, understanding non-verbal cues will be crucial in establishing whether the client is in the process of formulating a response or whether they are not going to respond at all.

3.7.3 Rescuing a Client From Silence

The problem with passive listening is that the client may not know if the solicitor has understood what is being said. If you find that an empty silence is impeding rather than promoting communication and you do nothing, the client may start to doubt whether you are actually interested. There are a number of ways to rescue a client from unhelpful silence by using prompts that interrupt the client's train of thought, accompanied by appropriate body language, such as making eye contact or nodding.

Examples of rescuing responses are, "Hmm", "I understand", "Okay", "Yes", or, "Go on". These types of responses from the solicitor will reassure the client that they are being listened to.

3.8 Active Listening

The edges between passive and active listening can be little blurred and there is a lack of consensus on where one ends and the other begins. The best way to approach this is that there are degrees of 'passive' and 'active' listening with overlapping areas in the middle.

Essentially, active listening is about being completely focused on the client's meaning. In contrast to passive listening (which also requires being completely focused), it also involves communicating to the speaker that their message has been received and understood. It can be demonstrated by re-phrasing what the client has said and giving something back to the client as a verbal response.

Active listening is a skill that can enable lawyers to improve their communication and rapport with their clients, increase client satisfaction, and improve the core business of preparing cases.

There is no universally accepted definition of active listening, but the term can be used to describe a more purposeful type of listening in certain contexts and typically involves the following:

1. Listening to verbal messages
2. Listening to non-verbal messages
3. Interpreting the feelings and intentions underlying what the client is saying (listening for emotion)
4. Demonstrating to a client that listening is taking place
5. Using appropriate but limited questioning to steer the client in the right direction

3.8.1 Demonstrating Active Listening by Responding Non-Verbally

The solicitor's response to what the client is saying may consist of non-verbal communication in the form of facial expressions, for example, frowning, wincing, or adopting a look of concern. Smiling can show a client that you are listening and following what they are saying, and a nod of the head can demonstrate a willingness to listen.

Body posture can also be used in conjunction with facial expressions to reflect back to the client that they are listening. Adopting an attentive posture, such as sitting forward or sideways on a chair with head tilted sideways, demonstrates that listening is taking place.

3.8.2 Demonstrating Active Listening by Responding Verbally

A verbal response is a more explicit way of demonstrating active listening and is perhaps easier for a client to understand. Responses can range from rescue phrases such as 'Please go on' to more involved responses which paraphrase what the client has just said or reflect back the emotions that the client is feeling. Paralanguage through vocal tone and pitch can also be used to convey to a client that you are interested in their story.

Here is an example of a more involved response which demonstrates active listening:

Client: "I couldn't believe he said that to me, like I was a piece of rubbish!"
Solicitor: "That must have been really upsetting for you. It's a very hurtful thing to say".

A client-centred approach includes knowing how to respond to the client's feelings. In order to do this, you need to be engaged in active listening. This involves showing you have understood not only the verbal words but also the underlying feelings and emotions. It is really important that clients feel they have been listened to. This is crucial in maintaining trust and confidence.

Consider the following example and work out the client's problem and the client's feelings.

Carla – "Shortly after we got married, my husband Tim and I decided to have wills drafted. I hadn't given making a will much thought. I'm only 38. Once we made the wills, I completely forgot about them. Then I got a call from Tim's work to say that he'd been taken to hospital. He had a brain haemorrhage and died three days later. I was totally overwhelmed. He was only 46. I couldn't believe it had happened. I've been worrying about money. I feel guilty about that. I don't know what I'm going to do. One minute, I think I'm okay, and the next, I can't stop crying. Tim has two children from his first marriage, and they phoned me last night and said they're not happy about the will and want to do something about it. I just can't believe this is all happening to me. It's like your worst nightmare".
Carla's problem – Carla's husband died unexpectedly, and she must now sort out the finances. The children from Tim's first marriage are contesting the will.
Carla's feelings – sadness, fear, stress, worry, shock, anger

Here is an example of two different approaches to a client's emotions.

Client: "I only bought the laptop a couple of months ago, and it's already running slow. I can't do anything on it. It just shuts down. It's rubbish".
Solicitor 1: "Did you have a written contract?"
Solicitor 2: "It must be frustrating to have spent all that money on something that doesn't work properly. Laptops are not cheap!"

Solicitor 1 ignores the emotions of the client and immediately takes complete control, forcing the client to answer questions set by the solicitor. The issue of whether there was a written contract would have come up at some point anyway and did not need to be raised at this stage. This approach may cause a client to become disengaged.

Solicitor 2 actively listens to the client's emotional message and the facts by responding back that the problem is about a faulty laptop and that the client is frustrated. The client will know that the solicitor has understood the client (not just the problem), and this will help to develop rapport, trust, and confidence between them, which in turn will encourage the client to talk.

3.9 Note-Taking

Naturally, you will need to make an accurate record of the information gathered during an interview together with any advice you have given, the client's decisions, and next steps. The question is how and when note-taking should take place. Head down, frenzied note-taking while a client is telling their story is likely to be very distracting and can result in damage to rapport caused by a lack of eye contact, but taking no notes is not advisable either (unless you have the audio equivalent to a photographic memory!).

There are two options. Firstly, use the first stage of the interview to listen without taking any notes, then use the questioning phase to fill gaps, probe for information, and take notes. This works well if you are blessed with a good memory. Alternatively, while the client is telling their story, you can take down very briefly the key points in a non-distracting way so that when you come to the questioning phase, you can use the key points as a framework.

It is worth explaining to a client at the outset that you will be taking notes during the interview, and in the concluding stages of the interview, the notes that you have taken should be summarised back to the client so that you can check that they are an accurate reflection of the information given.

In Summary

- Appreciate that listening and hearing serve very different functions, and that you need to be proficient in the skill of listening in client interviews.
- Appreciate that listening skills are often neglected and need to be developed.
- Understand the importance of professional listening, which requires a solicitor to be fully engaged throughout the encounter with the client.
- Ensure that you are familiar with the different levels of listening that can be used in an interview, namely passive and active listening.

- Understand the purpose of an open question in the listening phase of an interview.
- Recognise that active listening involves using body language and verbal responses to let the client know you are listening and understanding.
- Appreciate the importance of silence in the listening stage of the interview, but know when to rescue a client from ineffective silence if necessary.
- Understand the significance of non-verbal communication, such as facial expressions, body posture, and appearance during the listening phase.
- Develop a strategy for note-taking that does not distract a client and interrupt the flow of their story while enabling full and relevant information to be recorded.

Key Practice Case – A Complaint to the Legal Ombudsman (Anonymised)

Mr H instructed the firm to pursue a personal injury claim. Mr H's injuries and health conditions meant he found it difficult to read and write. He said he told the firm that they needed to communicate with him verbally, but they failed to do so.

Mr H felt that the firm had not supported him and complained that the firm failed to follow instructions as they continued to send him letters.

The outcome

The Legal Ombudsman decided that the firm's service was unreasonable as they did not handle Mr H's requests for reasonable adjustments as well as they could have. The firm knew of Mr H's condition from the start of the retainer, and although Mr H specifically asked for calls, this did not always happen.

It was accepted that some written correspondence would need to be sent to clients. However, the firm could have called Mr H to explain the contents of the letters that were being sent to him, which they did not always do. In those instances, Mr H had to chase them.

The evidence also showed that the firm delayed in telling Mr H about the additional support he could have received, such as a litigation friend.

The firm's service did not impact Mr H's claim, but it did affect his experience. Mr H experienced repeated inconvenience by having to chase the firm, but the impact of this was short-lived.

To remedy this, the Ombudsman proposed that the firm pay Mr H £250 compensation for the emotional impact.

Both the firm and Mr R accepted the Ombudsman's decision.

Practice Tips

- Before the interview, mentally prepare yourself to listen. Empty your mind of other matters and concerns so that you can focus on the task at hand and are able to give the client your undivided attention.
- Outside the pressures of the client interview, practice techniques for introductions and icebreakers with your network of family, friends, and colleagues.
- Try not to put pressure on yourself about icebreakers and building rapport. There is no 'one size fits all' approach, and with practice, you will find your own style of communication in the early stages of the interview.
- During the interview and in the listening phase, try to avoid interrupting the client or steering the narrative away from the direction the client wants it to go.
- Think about the most effective way for you to make notes during interviews.

Practice Risks

- Failing to listen to a client in an interview. This is detrimental to the client/solicitor relationship and the conduct of the legal matter/case generally.
- Neglecting to observe and understand non-verbal communication alongside verbal communication. This may result in the full message being lost
- Displaying negative body language will damage the client/solicitor relationship.
- Failing to give a client sufficient time to think about responses. This can derail their thought process and may elicit information which is much narrower and incomplete.

Exercises

EXERCISE A

Practise Passive and Active Listening

Do this exercise with a partner.

A. Divide into pairs: one speaker and one listener.
B. The speaker may choose an everyday subject to talk about for two minutes.

Phase 1: The speaker should tell their story to the listener. The listener must remain completely passive: Do not interrupt the speaker or ask any further questions. Keep your body posture and facial expressions as neutral as possible.

Phase 2: Repeat Phase 1, but this time with the listener responding normally and naturally to the story using any verbal and non-verbal behaviour that would usually be adopted.

Now, in the same pairs:

C. Discuss the different feelings/responses experienced by the speaker during each process.
D. Make a list of the different types of verbal and non-verbal behaviour used by the listener in Phase 2.

EXERCISE B

Reflect on Your Listening Skills

There is a tendency to understate the importance of listening in the process of communication, and this possibly stems from an incomplete understanding of the process itself. It gets overlooked in our day-to-day lives until such a time as we feel, perhaps, we have not been listened to. If we believe we are good listeners, there is little incentive to reflect and improve. We often mistakenly believe we are 'good' listeners when, in fact, the opposite is true.

Consider the following questions:

1. Do you let a speaker finish what they are saying before you speak?
2. While the speaker is still speaking, are you already formulating a response in your head?
3. Do you frame your responses in terms of what you have experienced? E.g., ' I had the same problem . . .'
4. Do you anticipate what the speaker is going to say?
5. Do you become easily distracted, leading to gaps in information?

We can probably all answer 'yes' to one or more of these questions. If you have answered 'yes' to some of these questions, then now is possibly a good time to think about how your listening skills can be developed and improved.

Self-Reflection Checklist

What three important things have you learn t from this chapter?	**1**	**2**	**3**
Set out the three additional steps that you need to take to learn the skills in this chapter in more detail.	**1**	**2**	**3**

References

Books

Doyle AC, *A Case of Mistaken Identity* (Solis Press 2011).

Hargie O and Dickson D, *Skilled Interpersonal: Communication Research, Theory and Practice* (Routledge 2005).

Kline JA, *Listening Effectively* (Air University Press 2008).

Murphy K, *You're Not Listening: What You're Missing and Why It Matters* (Vintage 2022).

Pease A and Pease B, *The Definitive Book of Body Language* (Orion 2016).

Reports

LexisNexis Bellwether Report 2015 Issue 3: The Age of the Client

Websites

www.sra.org.uk

4 Questioning Skills

Key Chapter Points

1. The listening phase of the interview is unlikely to provide all of the information that the solicitor will need to help a client.
2. The questioning phase enables the solicitor to probe more deeply about the information presented by the client in the listening phase.
3. The solicitor uses different questioning techniques to fill in gaps in the information, clear up ambiguities, and obtain any other facts needed to allow correct and relevant advice to be formulated.
4. Questions can be split into different types, which include open questions, closed questions, probing questions, and leading questions.
5. Using the correct type of question for the situation can help the solicitor obtain more and better-quality information.
6. Using an information funnel ensures that a complete picture is obtained by starting with open questions and then drilling down into the information using closed questions.
7. New information funnels should be opened up when necessary so that each separate facet of the client's narrative is exhausted.

4.1 Introduction

This chapter covers the questioning skills needed to move the interview on from the listening phase when the client has provided their story and the solicitor has been engaged in passive and active listening. By this point, the solicitor should have a basic idea of the client's problem, but there may be significant gaps that need to be filled. Different forms of questions can now be utilised to maximise information gathering. The skill of questioning in a client interview is simply about asking the right questions at the right time!

This chapter will cover the importance of questioning in the initial client interview, questioning skills that must be demonstrated by candidates in the SQE2 interviewing assessment, different questioning techniques, how they should be utilised, and the tasks that are involved in the questioning phase of the interview.

DOI: 10.4324/9781003519096-4

4.2 Questioning in the Interview

Questioning as a skill is developed at an early age, and anyone who has spent any length of time with toddlers will have experienced the incessant and repetitive use of "why?' as they make sense of their world and begin to practice their social and problem-solving skills. With the exception of teenagers (whose interpersonal communication is often reduced to self-conscious, one-syllable responses), questioning is a key part of everyday life and is the basis of most interpersonal encounters. For professionals, it is an essential facet of problem-solving and decision-making.

In the context of the initial client interview, even if all the listening techniques discussed in Chapter 3 are utilised, it is still unlikely that sufficient information will have been obtained for a solicitor to meet the objectives of the interview. Rarely are clients able to neatly sort into mental pigeonholes the relevant facts that the solicitor will need and irrelevant facts that the solicitor will not need. They may forget to include key details when they are telling their story, or there may be areas that are unclear and need further explanation.

Here is a reminder of the interview objectives:

1. Build a rapport with the client to enable a professional relationship to be formed.
2. Find out why the client has come and identify the legal issue.
3. Identify and understand the client's goals relating to the legal issue.
4. Gather relevant information to be able to provide at least some basic advice on the legal position and the range of options available to achieve the client's goals.
5. Help the client so that they are able to make an informed decision about what they need and what the options are.
6. Agree on a plan for future action or basic steps to move the matter forward.

In the questioning phase (when a more active role is assumed), the solicitor should aim to:

- Question to fill in gaps or provide more detail.
- Question for understanding or resolving misunderstanding.
- Sum up and communicate understanding of the facts back to the client.
- Check for the client's agreement to understanding the facts.
- Amend understanding of facts if incorrectly understood.

4.3 Questioning Skills in SQE2

Within the SQE2 interviewing assessment, the skill assessed is:

> Listen to the client and use questioning effectively to enable the client to tell the solicitor what is important to them.

The indicators demonstrating competency are:

- The candidate asks appropriate questions (e.g., questions designed to elicit relevant information from the client).
- The candidate uses a combination of open and closed questions. An open question is a question which invites the client to share more detailed information, e.g., it could be a question beginning with the words "tell me about the property you would like to buy . . ." Closed questions could be questions where the response would be "yes" or "no", e.g., "Do you own your own property?").

Indicators that do not demonstrate competency are:

- The candidate does not ask appropriate or relevant questions.
- The candidate uses only closed questions or does not use sufficient/appropriate open questions, which prevents the client from explaining what is important to them.

You can access the full performance indicators for the client SQE2 interview assessment here:

https://sqe.sra.org.uk/docs/default-source/pdfs/sqe2-sample-questions/int-performance-indicators.pdf?sfvrsn=69961d98_2

4.4 The Foundations of Legal Questioning

When we think of legal questioning, the first type that probably springs to mind is in the context of advocacy and the forensic task of questioning in court. However, if you cast your mind back to Chapter 2, you will remember that we described interviewing as a foundational skill within the set of oral legal skills that a legal professional needs and it is within the context of the interview that the skill of questioning is first learned. The style of questioning that takes place in an interview is very different from the theatre of the courtroom. There are some basic rules to follow for effective questioning, and these are as follows.

Questions should be structured in a way that a client can understand. They should be clear, concise, and unambiguous. If you are unable to express the question in a straightforward way, then the client will become confused, and you may undermine rapport.

For closed questions (which we discuss in more detail in section 4.8), there should be one question at a time rather than several questions combined into one long question with multiple parts. This is likely to result in a client losing their train of thought.

Once you have asked a question, avoid the temptation to jump in too soon. A mistake that is very often made is to assume that a client has not understood, but a premature reaction on the part of the solicitor could derail the client's thought process. Give the client sufficient time to think and formulate an answer. Be observant of non-verbal cues, and only if a client is struggling with the question should you step in.

Be conscious of your own non-verbal cues and ask questions at an appropriate pace, avoiding legal jargon.

4.5 Question Aims

The questioning phase is not just about filling in gaps in information and clearing up ambiguities (although that is, of course, hugely important). The aims of the questioning phase can be summarised as follows:

- Steer the interview in the right direction
- Fill in gaps in information and clear up ambiguities efficiently
- Demonstrate concern/interest
- Ascertain attitudes/feelings/opinions
- Encourage participation
- Clarify the client's objectives

4.6 Asking the Right Questions – Preparation and Response

During the questioning phase, the solicitor shapes the interview and uses degrees of control to steer it in the right direction, but the direction taken is dependent on whether the solicitor has used effective listening skills in the listening phase. A failure to listen properly will become evident to a client once the questioning phase begins if, rather than filling in gaps, the solicitor is asking for information already provided. This could result in a loss of solicitor credibility and damage to rapport. It can be difficult when under pressure to think about what the relevant questions are, but listening very carefully to what a client is saying will help to guide you to the next question that needs to be asked.

The amount and quality of information obtained and the client's engagement in the process of questioning will, to a large degree, depend on the type of questions asked. Thoughtful and careful preparation is required by the solicitor to elicit a specific response from the client. In simple terms, the solicitor needs to ask well-crafted questions using appropriate techniques in the correct order.

During the listening phase of the interview, the solicitor should make a list of the areas that need elaboration so that the list can be used to formulate relevant questions in the questioning phase.

4.7 Types of Questions

There are several different questioning techniques which can be used during the interview, depending on the quality of the information received during the listening phase. The types of questions used will range from open to leading, with the type of question at any given time widening or narrowing the zone of information obtained from the client. Open questions leave the response wide open, whereas leading questions provide very restricted responses with little room for manoeuvre.

It is important to understand the different forms of questions and their uses before considering how to use them.

4.8 The First Question

After the meet, greet, and seat phase of the interview, the solicitor needs to establish the reason for the client's appointment. This should be done using a closed question before moving on to the first open question, which is used to encourage the client to tell their story.

4.9 Open Questions

As we saw in Chapter 3, open questions are basic introductory questions intended to encourage the client to talk but also to enable the client to determine the parameters and direction of the interview for themselves. The client is given the opportunity to say what the problem really is from their own perspective, and they can explain what they need or want, or don't want, in their own words.

Open questions work well with clients who like to talk but do not always work well with clients who are not comfortable controlling the narrative, who are having difficulty with recall or memory, or who simply do not know where to start. In these circumstances, a client will need scaffolding to encourage them to talk, and this can be achieved by narrowing the field of the open question slightly so that the client has an idea of where to begin. Another problem that could be encountered with an open question is that it may elicit a response that is irrelevant and the solicitor will have to re-assess how to get to the relevant information using a different open question.

Open questions can be very useful in getting clients to talk about very sensitive issues by allowing them to have control over the disclosure.

Open questions can range from very wide to less wide (but not so narrow as to be a closed question). Here are some examples:

- Tell me about . . . ? (A very wide question which could result in a large amount of information)

- Tell me what happened on that day. (Restricted to information about one day)
- Tell me what happened before the meeting. (Restricted to information about before the meeting)
- Tell me what was said during the meeting. (Restricted to what was said during the meeting)

4.10 Probing Responses

Probing questions can be used to supplement a client's response by taking them through areas of their story that they need to develop. A number of probing techniques are discussed here.

4.10.1 Interrogatory

The simplest form of probing question is an interrogatory question which is intended to elicit a deeper insight into a situation. An example might be "What made you think that?" or, "How did you feel then?" These can be useful in moving the story to a deeper level of analysis while retaining the features of open questions.

4.10.2 Keyword

Keyword questions are another type of question designed to elicit more information from a client. In a keyword question, the solicitor repeats the client's words to get them to focus and enlarge on them. It relies on proficient listening skills to hook a keyword and then repeat it to the client within a question. It is also useful in reinforcing to the client that you are actively listening to them by mirroring their language.

For example, imagine the following dialogue is part of an interview with a personal injury client:

Client: I wasn't really sure what was going on at first, as I was busy washing Mrs Birch, who had spilt her cornflakes, but then the hoist swung round and hit me on my lower back.
Solicitor: You say it swung round and hit your lower back?
Client: Yes, really hard, hard enough to knock me off my feet!

4.10.3 Reflective

Reflective questions are a form of probing question that can be used to focus on a keyword and link the client's thought process to the next crucial piece of information, for example:

> "How did you feel then?"

4.11 Closed Questions

Closed questions are used to elicit a specific piece of information, for example, a yes/no response or an answer restricted to discrete facts. They are generally unhelpful in the beginning stages of the interview because they will result in limited information from the client, and you may end up running out of time or running overtime trying to backtrack and get all of the relevant facts.

Closed questions should be used after open questions have obtained sufficient information to enable you to work out what else you need. That information can then be dealt with by asking a closed question.

Here are some examples of closed questions:

- Can you tell me the colour of the car?
- Was it raining that night?
- How fast was the car going?

Closed questions are a time-efficient way to get straight to the information required, and this is important in a busy legal practice when there is limited time for interviews. They can also motivate clients because they can be much easier to answer, can prompt a client to recall forgotten information, and can pull back a client who is talking too much.

However, asking too many closed questions in quick succession can start to feel rather like an interrogation, and the process becomes more of a mechanical questionnaire-filling exercise, which may damage rapport and the client/solicitor relationship. Other disadvantages of closed questions are that they can result in whole areas of relevant information being missed, and they can deny a client the chance to tell their story in their own way. The solicitor also needs to take care that closed questions do not pressurise a client into answering in a certain way, resulting in accuracy of information being affected.

Here is an example of how two questions (one opened and one closed) about the same matter could elicit a different response:

Solicitor 1: Can you tell me how he was behaving?
Solicitor 2: Was he angry?

4.12 The Effective Leading Question

Leading questions are a form of closed questions which already contain the information you want and also give or suggest the answer to the client.

If we take the examples from 4.7, these would be re-worded as follows:

- Can you tell me the colour of the car? – It was a red car, wasn't it?
- Was it raining that night? – It was raining that night, wasn't it?
- How fast was the car going? – It was going over 50 miles per hour, correct?

The answers to these leading questions clearly imply that 'yes' is the anticipated answer. The client has, therefore, been 'led' to the answer without having to think independently about the response. For that reason, you should be very careful about the use of leading questions, particularly in respect of contentious matters. If you have prompted your client's answer in respect to a contentious issue, you will need to look for independent verification of the information.

Leading questions can, however, be useful in piecing together the client's problem when a communication barrier is encountered. For example, if a client is reluctant to disclose information of a deeply personal nature, such as a sexual matter, a leading question is a signal to the client that the solicitor already knows some of the background information and is not judging the client. It is safe for the client to proceed.

4.13 Order and Knowledge Transfer – The Information Funnel

So far, in this chapter, we have explored the different questioning techniques that can be used to obtain information. We now consider in what order the questions should be asked. The starting point is that if we decide to use only open questions or closed questions, we are unlikely to obtain all of the information that is needed to move on to the advising phase of the interview.

Most literature on the topic of questioning recommends asking questions in a 'funnel' sequence, starting with open questions until they are no longer producing relevant information and then drilling down to find out specific facts and missing details using closed questions as we near the end of a particular line of questioning. Using the funnel approach to gathering information gives the best chance that all of the relevant information will be obtained as efficiently as possible.

It may be necessary to use more than one information 'funnel' during questioning; for example, in a personal injury claim, there may be a need to open up separate funnels dealing with different types of information, such as the events leading up to the accident, then the happening of the accident, then the aftermath, then the injury and so on. Of course, the order of the funnels will depend on the client's initial narrative and might not follow a linear pattern.

Here is an example of how a funnel can be used in a personal injury matter involving an accident in a supermarket:

1. Tell me what happened from the time when you went into the shop.
2. What happened next?
3. Which aisle was that?
4. Which shelf did it fall from?
5. Where did it hit you?
6. How did you land?
7. Did you feel any pain?

In Summary

- Appreciate that the listening phase of the interview is unlikely to result in all of the information needed to advise a client.
- Understand the importance of the questioning phase of the interview in meeting the objectives of the interview.
- Understand the continuing importance of rapport, trust, and confidence during the questioning phase of the interview.
- Ensure that you have used listening skills effectively so that appropriate and effective questioning techniques can be used.
- Understand the significance of the different types of questions and when it is appropriate to use each type during an interview.
- Know when and how to use the information funnel sequence to obtain all of the key information, starting with open questions and moving on to closed questions to get at the essential specifics.
- Appreciate the situations when it is not going to be appropriate to use leading questions within an interview.

Key Practice Cases: Complaints to the Legal Ombudsman (Anonymised)

1. Miss E – Delays and poor service

Miss E decided to have a will drafted and instructed solicitors to help her draft it. She found the firm online and instructed them on the basis that, on their website, they promised a quick, efficient service. However, she soon started to experience problems contrary to what the website promised. Miss E claimed that the firm had:

- Delayed in drafting the will;
- Failed to keep her informed about progress;
- Continued to work on matters and request information after she had told them that she did not want them to continue working (they only stopped contacting her after she had paid some of their fees); and
- Drafted a will that contained errors in it.

Miss E complained to the firm on a number of occasions, but they failed to respond. She then brought her complaint to the Ombudsman, who found that the firm had delayed drafting the will and also delayed in responding to Miss E's queries. They sent numerous drafts of the will, often containing errors. They also failed to address Miss E's complaint despite her chasing for a response. An investigator suggested to both Miss E and the firm that a fair and reasonable remedy to her complaint would be compensation of £250, with any outstanding costs to be deducted from this amount. The firm agreed, and Miss F also accepted this as a fair resolution.

2. Mr F – Failure to follow instructions

Mr F's mother passed away. In her will, she had left shares which were to be sold with the profits going to her estate. Solicitors were instructed by the executors, Mr F and his sister, to sell the shares. In principle, this would be a relatively straightforward process for a firm of experienced probate lawyers. However, it took them three years to execute the will and to distribute the estate. Eventually, the firm paid the estate £6,000, which it claimed were the dividends of the share sale. But Mr F was sceptical about whether the shares had, in fact, been sold. When he questioned the firm and asked for a receipt of the sale, it was unable to meet his request. Mr F then escalated his complaint to the Legal Ombudsman.

When the complaint was investigated, the Ombudsman found that the firm had not even sold the shares but had instead paid the estate using their own funds. They then tried to justify this by stating that they had calculated what the shares would have been worth. However, when an investigator scrutinised the figures, it became apparent that they had miscalculated and underpaid Mr F by some £4,000. The investigator agreed on a way of resolving the issue mutually by getting the firm to pay Mr F £1,000 for distress and inconvenience, reimburse their costs, and finally, provide him with the share certificates so he could sell the shares. Although the firm claimed it was an honest mistake, they were reported by the Ombudsman to the SRA for potential misconduct

Practice Tips

- Take time to reflect and check the notes that you have taken before embarking on the questioning phase of the interview.
- Keep track of time while questioning, but do not rush either the asking of the questions or responses from the client.
- Try to avoid rolling multiple questions into one question to the client as this will cause confusion, and it will be difficult for a client to unravel precisely what information you actually want from them.

- Remember to keep your questions short and clear, as vague questions will be difficult for a client to understand.
- Try to understand what a client is saying instead of thinking about the next question.
- Practise using good-quality opening questions for a range of situations.

Practice Risks

- Asking only closed questions during an interview is very unlikely to elicit all of the information needed and will waste interview time.
- Asking more than one question at a time will confuse a client and derail their train of thought.
- A lack of thought and care in the types of questions asked will impact on the client/solicitor relationship.
- Failure to make brief notes during the listening phase will make it very difficult to know how to approach the questioning phase of the interview.

Exercises

EXERCISE A

Read the following conversation between a client and solicitor and:

- Identify the types of questions used
- Analyse the effects of each question
- Consider an alternative questioning approach

1. Solicitor: Please take a seat Mr Clarke.
2. Client: Thank you very much.
3. Solicitor: Right now, Mr Clarke, how can I help?
4. Client: Er, it's a long story, and I don't really know where to start.
5. Solicitor: All right, if I can just go through a few initial questions with you then. I understand a claim has been made against you by Bathright for non-payment of a bill. Is that correct?
6. Client: Yes, that's right.
7. Solicitor: It's for £16,000?
8. Client: Yes.
9. Solicitor: Why didn't you pay for the bathroom? Were you overcharged? Couldn't you afford to pay?
10. Client: No.
11. Solicitor: Can you tell me what happened?
12. Client: Well, back in April.

13. Solicitor: Last year?
14. Client: No, this year. I saw an advert in the local paper saying . . .
15. Solicitor: *The Messenger* or the *Evening News*?
16. Client: In *The Messenger*, saying. . .

EXERCISE B

Mrs Khan's marriage has broken down after 20 years, and she decides to seek legal advice about a divorce. She has a severe visual impairment but does not want anyone to know that she is thinking about a divorce, so she wants to meet with a solicitor by herself.

You are a solicitor in a local firm that deals with family law. What steps would you take to arrange a suitable appointment for Mrs Khan, and what factors would you consider?

Self-Reflection Checklist

What three important things have you learnt from this chapter?	**1**	**2**	**3**
Set out the three additional steps that you need to take to learn the skills in this chapter in more detail.	**1**	**2**	**3**

5 Analysis, Explanation, and Advice

Key Chapter Points

1. The final phase of the interview is the culmination of all the hard work carried out during the listening and questioning phases and involves giving back meaningful information to the client.
2. In this final stage, the solicitor summarises the key points of the client's story and seeks their confirmation before completing a preliminary analysis of the matter.
3. Information can then be given to the client, including explanations of client care matters, explanations of legal rules, legal and non-legal options, advice, and a plan of action/next steps.
4. Giving advice will involve on-the-spot critical thinking and problem-solving so that the legal position can be correctly applied to a client's situation.
5. Any advice given must be accurate and communicated in a way that clients can understand, particularly in relation to individual attributes, needs, and circumstances.
6. There may be circumstances when it is not appropriate to give definitive advice during the initial interview, and the client should be informed of the reasons why this is not possible.
7. The client and the solicitor should agree on the plan of action/next steps before the interview is brought to an end.

5.1 Introduction

With the listening and questioning phases of the interview complete, the client and solicitor now embark on the final phases of the interview journey. During this section, the solicitor completes the analysis of the information so that explanations and advice, if appropriate, can be provided to the client.

This chapter covers the final steps of the interview and the process of giving information to the client so as to maximise understanding. It also examines the very last steps that are needed to draw the interview to a close effectively.

DOI: 10.4324/9781003519096-5

5.2 Final Steps

What follows are suggestions on steps that you can take during the final phase of the interview:

- Summarise and seek agreement from the client on key parts of the information disclosed
- Complete the analysis of the information supplied
- Provide the client with explanations
- State advice and/or plan of action
- Repeat advice/plan of action AND check for the client's agreement or amend if necessary
- Discuss follow-up work to be done by the client
- Discuss follow-up work to be done by the solicitor
- State the next contact between the solicitor and the client
- Ask if the client has any further questions and answer them
- Goodbyes

5.3 Analysing Information and the Wider Legal Context

While the listening and questioning phases of the interview are taking place, the solicitor is also:

- Taking notes,
- Sorting through the information provided by the client,
- Sifting out the relevant facts,
- Analysing which of the legal rules and principles within the solicitor's framework of knowledge are relevant to the facts provided, and
- Applying legal rules and principles to the facts.

This process should be familiar territory for law students and solicitors alike because legal education programmes generally include assessments that test students' analytical skills through problem-type questions. Law students will probably be well versed in the methods designed to help with legal analysis in academic studies, such as IRAC or ILAC.

The difficulty, though, especially for an inexperienced solicitor, is that the facts presented in an exam problem question are constructed around clear and established legal principles, and there is a neat solution against which a student's performance is assessed. In a real client interview, the solicitor may be faced with a jumble of facts that do not fit neatly into a legal category within the solicitor's knowledge framework, and the use of IRAC or a similar method of analysis does not provide much help.

The problem presented in a real interview is one of immediacy. The interview is happening face-to-face and in real time. Even in a simulated interview assessment, a student is provided with some relevant information, instructions, and time to prepare, but in a real interview, a solicitor is expected to obtain and process large amounts of information and be ready to give something back to the client without the luxury of time for quiet contemplation. Understandably, the advising and explaining phase of the interview can be overwhelming for the interviewer, but it is the focal point for the client and probably the main point of the interview from their perspective, so it is crucial that it is carried out with proficiency.

Use of the listening and questioning techniques discussed in Chapters 3 and 4 will naturally integrate some thinking time into the process. During this time, the solicitor can form an initial impression about the legal issue or issues and possible advice. It is a good idea at this point, before proceeding to the information-giving phase, to summarise and seek agreement from the client on key aspects of their story and confirm the client's goals. The solicitor should then have a very clear understanding of the facts and what the client wants so that the advice or explanations given are appropriate. An example of how this can be approached is as follows:

> "Before we discuss what can be done, I would like to just check with you that I have fully understood".

5.4 What Is Involved in Legal Analysis?

Once the solicitor has sifted through factual information provided by the client for relevancy and filled in gaps through questioning, the final stages of the interview involve a process of legal analysis.

The object of legal analysis is to arrive at a solution for clients. It is, therefore, very closely interlinked with problem-solving. Legal analysis involves analysing the facts and information presented by a client to determine the following:

A. The exact nature of the client's legal problem or question
B. The legal context in which the problem or question sits
C. The law (or other system) that governs the legal problem of question
D. How the law that governs the legal issue applies to the facts
E. What, if any, legal remedy is available
F. Whether any of the legal remedies will meet the client's goals and objectives.

5.5 Explaining the Way Forward

Having spent time telling their story, the client will now expect input from the solicitor. Failure to handle this stage of the interview with care could result in damage to the client/solicitor relationship. After all, the client has been persuaded to talk openly and has possibly revealed their innermost thoughts and feelings, so it is important that they are given something in exchange.

Before a client makes a decision and gives instructions (if appropriate at this stage), there are likely to be a number of other matters that need to be carefully explained, but the exact information will largely depend on the type of legal matter.

It is sensible at this stage to take a few moments to set out for the client what is going to happen next in the interview, i.e., you will deal with any client care matters, and then you will explain some key points about the type of matter and the client's legal position, provide advice (if appropriate) and/or next steps that will be needed.

5.6 Relevant Procedures

Clients will need an explanation of legal procedures that will have to be followed in their type of matter.

Transactional matters such as domestic conveyancing will involve explanations of stages of the process, documents required from the client, and general timescales. There may also be a need for case-specific explanations, for example, if the client has provided information about a planning issue.

Matters involving contentious areas of law may need a different approach and are likely to involve information on the nature of the legal issue presented by the facts, followed by details of the relevant law and the client's legal position within that framework, together with what a client must prove, evidence likely to be required, stages of litigation, risks of litigation, possible complications, legal options and any non-legal alternatives (such as ADR).

It is important to manage clients' expectations from the very beginning by providing realistic information on how long the process is likely to take and the possibility of delays or problems arising.

If any risks have been identified, a record should be kept so that if the client instructs you to act, you are able to monitor the risk levels and keep the client updated.

5.7 Advising

Providing legal advice to clients is, in many ways, regarded as the central purpose of the interview and the main service provided by solicitors. The academic and skills stages of legal education will have prepared new entrants to the legal professions for this part of the role to some extent, and it is an area that even inexperienced legal professionals should be reasonably familiar with.

The construction of advice in legal education is one of the major skills which is actually taught at the degree and professional qualification stages, although usually in the context of advice in a written form, for example, in a letter to a client.

What you will need to provide to the client is an outline of the relevant legal rule or principle and an explanation of all legal and non-legal options that are appropriate, the advantages and disadvantages for each option, and steps that will need to be taken for each option.

5.7.1 General Principles

Here are some steps to give clients effective advice:

- Make sure that you have finished the acquiring information phase before you start giving advice to a client.
- The advice that you give should include what the client wants from the interview. Even if what the client wants is unrealistic (for example, 'I want £1,000,000 for my whiplash claim, and I won't accept a penny less!'), you need to be able to address it. You would have to carefully and diplomatically explain to the client how damages are assessed in the UK.
- The advice that you give must be accurate. If you are unsure of any aspect, do not be afraid to inform the client that you will undertake some research and will provide advice at a later date.

5.7.2 Specific Client Advice

A client may expect to receive very specific advice at the conclusion of the interview. This could relate, for example, to a procedural timescale or definitive answer to whether they will 'win' their case. Avoid giving a strong indication of the client's case in these circumstances. It is perfectly acceptable to explain to a client that you are unable to provide strong indications or certainties, particularly in transactions and contentious matters where there are so many variables that can affect timescales and prospects of success.

If you are in a position to give a client specific advice during the interview, this should be repeated to the client, and they should be asked for confirmation of their understanding of the advice.

While you are not assessed on the law within the SQE2 interview, it goes without saying that any legal advice given in a real interview must be accurate.

5.7.3 Should We Advise in Interviews?

In the context of a real-life interview, giving advice involves using critical and reflective problem-solving skills and sometimes innovative solutions through the application of the law to the client's problem. However, new solicitors may experience a number of challenges when trying to formulate on-the-spot advice for a client. Even experienced solicitors may struggle with the immediacy of the task in tricky cases.

Here are some of the challenges that can be experienced by inexperienced legal professionals:

1. Unfamiliarity with the area of law/aspects of the topic have been forgotten
2. Problems translating academic knowledge of a legal topic into real, practical advice
3. Difficulty translating legal concepts into plain English
4. No real experience of how black letter law translates into legal procedures and other practical consequences, including costs
5. Unfamiliarity with non-legal options which may be more appropriate for the client than legal options.

As we suggested in 5.4.2, if you are unsure about giving advice, it is much better to inform the client that advice will be provided at a later date.

Here are some additional factors that could affect the decision to give advice at the interview:

(i) Legal Jargon

Effectively communicating advice is central to the client/solicitor relationship. The main aim of giving the client advice at this stage is so that they leave the interview having gained a basic understanding of the legal position. If this is to be achieved, then the process of translation of legal jargon that we described in Chapter 2 must be adopted confidently, concisely, and accurately.

Legal matters need to be explained in ordinary language. If for any reason this is not possible within the interview setting, then you should re-assess whether to give advice at this point.

(ii) Client Understanding

Even if you have provided objectively clear and understandable advice and explanations, there may be a number of reasons why a client is having difficulties understanding the advice. The legal issue necessitating legal advice may be one that is deeply upsetting to a client and is affecting their ability to process advice given at this point.

(iii) Speed Kills

You may have only up to an hour or so to conduct an initial client interview. As you reach the final stages of the interview, you may find that you are running out of time, and the temptation is to rattle through the legal advice phase at such a speed that the client ends up completely bewildered. If you are running out of time and there are lengthy or complex issues to be explained, re-assess whether it is appropriate to do so at this point.

(iv) Client Recall

Obviously, you cannot give meaningful and accurate advice to a client when you do not have all the relevant facts. If, during the acquiring information phase, the client is having problems recalling key information, you should explain that you will not be able to give advice until such information has been obtained. Likewise, if you are able to give advice during the interview but the client is having trouble recalling the advice, you may decide that the advice should be given in writing instead.

(v) Ethics and Compliance

The Law Society Practice Note of 8 September 2021 sets out the client care information requirements for new clients. Much of the information is provided once there is a contract (retainer) in place, and it will be included in a client care letter. However, it is important to remember Paragraph 8.6 CCS, which applies during the initial client interview and which sets out that solicitors must give clients information in a way they can understand and ensure they are in a position to make informed decisions about the services they need, how their matter will be handled and the options available to them.

It is also important to remember the obligations in CCS 3.4 and CCF 4.2, which require solicitors and firms to take into account a client's attributes, needs, and circumstances. This is acknowledging, on a regulatory level, that each client is unique and must be treated as an individual.

There will be routine transactional matters where it is appropriate to give detailed advice, for example, in a domestic house sale, but in other matters, it may not be possible or appropriate to give specific advice until further information has been obtained or you have had an opportunity to research the law.

5.7.4 Helping the Client Decide

If you have given the client a range of legal and/or non-legal options to resolve a legal problem or to deal with a transactional issue, it is your responsibility to help them decide what option is going to be the best one, in terms of achieving the client's objective. This does not mean making the decision for them. This would not align with a client-centred approach. Instead, what is required is accurate information of advantages, disadvantages, timescales, risks, and costs relevant to the client's aims and objectives so that the client can reach a decision for themselves. A client may ask the solicitor to recommend one of the options that has been explained. The best way to approach this is to involve the client as much as possible in making the decision for themselves by asking what they think about the options and if they have a particular preference in view of their own goals and needs.

5.8 Plan of Action/Next Steps

A client-centred approach to interviewing enables and encourages clients to actively participate in all stages of the process, and it is in the final stages that you can enlist the client to be involved in the progress of the matter.

The plan or next steps to be taken by both parties will depend on a number of factors. A client may not wish the solicitor to do anything else for the time being, perhaps because they want to speak to a relative or are undecided about whether to proceed with instructions.

If the client does wish to proceed, there may be matters of further information or documents that they need to provide to the solicitor, and a timescale for the client to provide such information should be agreed. Likewise, a timescale for matters that the solicitor will attend to should be set out clearly for the client.

Any external deadlines, such as the fast-approaching expiry of limitation periods, should be explained to the client as well as the necessary steps to protect the client's position.

The solicitor should check with the client how they wish to be contacted by the solicitor, and the client should be provided with direct contact details for the solicitor and the best way to reach them.

If advice is to be given to a client in writing, the client should be informed when they can expect to receive the advice or any other follow-up communications.

5.9 Closing the Interview

The interview should end with the client feeling listened to, respected, and provided with sufficient information pertaining to the problem.

As you move towards the closure of the interview, there are some strategies that you can use to bring it to an end professionally and smoothly.

Remember that a client may have been recalling and discussing difficult or sensitive information and may be feeling the emotional effects, so the interview needs to be brought to an end gently.

It might be helpful to recap the next steps or plan of action at this point. This often signals to a client that the interview is naturally about to end. Give the client a final opportunity to ask any questions or raise any concerns.

In the same way as we can use small talk at the beginning of the interview, it can also be integrated into the final stages. Again, this will put a client on notice that the interview is concluding. Make sure, however, that the small talk is authentic.

Finally, remember to end the interview politely by helping the client with their coat/bags, accompanying them out of the room and back to reception, and then saying goodbye.

In Summary

- Ensure that you have completed the acquiring information phase of the interview before proceeding to the explanation and advice phase.
- Check that you have correctly understood the key points with the client before proceeding.
- Analyse the information received and begin to sort it into your framework of legal knowledge so that you can apply the legal rules/principles to your client's facts.
- Each interview experience is unique, and you need to decide whether it is appropriate to give legal advice during the initial interview, taking into account your own legal knowledge framework, the quality of the disclosure, and your client's attributes, needs, and considerations.
- Only give advice if it is appropriate to do so and you are confident that the advice you are giving is accurate.
- Take particular care to avoid using legal jargon during the advice phase of the interview, as you need to ensure that clients understand the advice they have been given.
- Ensure that you are concluding the interview with a plan of action and that both parties are clear about who is doing what.
- Integrate some small talk into the final stage of the interview so that the rapport established during the interview is reinforced.

Key Practice Case – The Scope and Limits of Legal Duty and Professional Advice

Miller v Irwin Mitchell LLP [2024] ***EWCA Civ 53***

Facts

The claimant (C) sustained personal injuries on 13 May 2014 while on holiday and called the defendant's (D) legal helpline on 19 May 2014 after seeing a television advertisement. A helpline adviser (H) gave C some general advice about personal injury claims and referred the matter to D's travel litigation group. The group requested further details from C, which she provided on 8 April 2015. In November 2015, C underwent an amputation of her lower leg. In January 2016, D sent C a conditional fee agreement to sign.

D then sent a letter of claim to the tour operator, requesting that it notify its insurers immediately. The insurer declined cover on the basis that the tour operator had failed to comply with the notification provisions in its insurance policy. In July 2016, the tour operator went into administration. D concluded that there was no prospect of recovery from the insurer and notified C. She sued for professional negligence on the basis that she had entered into an express or implied retainer with D when she first spoke to H, alternatively that D owed her an equivalent duty of care in tort

Held

The judge at the trial held that there had been no express or implied retainer, or any like tortious duty of care, from that time, and that D had been under no duty to advise C to notify the tour operator of the accident prior to the sending of the letter of claim.

Appeal

C appealed against the order dismissing her claim for damages for professional negligence against D in respect of the conduct of her personal injury claim. C submitted that H, by specifically advising her about the limitation period for bringing a claim against the tour operator, had voluntarily assumed responsibility for advising her on steps to take to safeguard against the risk that the tour operator's insurer would not cover liability to pay her claim.

The appeal was dismissed. The Court of Appeal held that a legal helpline advisor who gave preliminary legal advice on limitation to a prospective client did not thereby assume a duty to advise on all steps to protect the client's position, such as notifying a potential defendant of an accident. The advice on limitation did not imply that there was nothing else the claimant needed to do; it was simply preliminary general advice.

The case illustrates the vital importance of defining from the outset the scope and limits of a professional's duty of care (in this case, a solicitor) when giving preliminary advice to a prospective client and where there is no engagement letter.

Practice Tips

- Take a few moments between the acquiring of information phase and the advising phase to gather your thoughts. Explain to the client that you will be moving on to the next phase and ask them if they would like a quick break before proceeding.
- The final discussions that take place in the interview can be easily forgotten, so it is a good idea to make a note of the explanations and advice that you have given to the client.
- After the interview, speak to a colleague about any elements that you are unsure about.
- Prepare the file note as soon as you possibly can, but certainly within 24 hours of the meeting. Memories can quickly fade, and you do not want to

be in a position where you have to contact the client for information that they have already provided.

- Immediately diarise any follow-ups that have been agreed upon with the client and also external deadlines that may apply.

Practice Risks

- Failing to prepare a file note of the interview in a timely fashion will impact on the client/solicitor relationship as facts are quickly forgotten, and it may be necessary to revert back to the client.
- Failing to diarise any immediate steps that need to be taken will have a detrimental impact on the conduct of the case.
- Giving legal advice when you are unsure about whether it is accurate risks the credibility of the solicitor and impacts on the client/solicitor relationship.
- Neglecting to terminate the interview appropriately can affect the rapport between the client and the solicitor.

Exercises

EXERCISE A

How would explain the following legal terms to a client using plain English?

- Abstract of title
- Assured shorthold tenancy
- Beneficiary
- Chattels
- Disbursement
- Executor
- Grants of representation
- *Ex turpi causa non oritur actio*
- Lasting power of attorney
- Restrictive covenant

Practise translating legal terminology into plain English with a partner and check their understanding of your explanations.

EXERCISE B

Identify the Legal Problem and the Emotions

Read the following extract and identify the relevant legal problem and the client's emotions.

Client: It's not really about compensation. I just want an apology. My life has been turned upside down by all of this, and it's just so unfair. You're supposed to be able to trust your GP, and I think he needs to be struck off so that he can't do this to any other patients. I'd hate for anyone else to have to go through this. I mean, I must have gone four or five times with stomach pains before I was referred to the hospital and diagnosed with cancer, and by then, the tumour was too difficult to operate on.

Self-Reflection Checklist

What three important things have you learnt from this chapter?	**1**	**2**	**3**
Set out the three additional steps that you need to take to learn the skills in this chapter in more detail.	**1**	**2**	**3**

Reference

Case

Miller v Irwin Mitchell LLP [2024] EWCA Civ 53

6 When Things Go Wrong

Key Chapter Points

1. This chapter provides the reader with a range of guides designed to assist in those circumstances where the smooth running of the interview is interrupted by factors either within or outside the interviewer's control.
2. The process of completing a legal interview is one that is subject to the intricacies of human behaviour, and it is therefore important to ensure that a person new to the process is able to recognise the issue and to adopt approaches to ensure that the interview is returned to a smooth and professional part of the legal process.
3. A competent legal professional carries out their role to the expected standards as set out by professional bodies and associated codes.
4. From the requirement to be constantly self-reflective through to the need to ensure that the interviewer themselves is aiding the smooth conduct of the appointment, the chapter consider the internal processes of the legal professional and how they can go awry.
5. The chapter also looks to provide the interviewer with a wide range of client-centred obstacles to the completion of the interview. We identify the signs and look to provide a range of strategies that can assist in dealing with everything from a lack of engagement to dealing with conflict, aggression, or emotion.
6. There is recognition of the toll that interviewing can take upon legal professionals themselves. Many areas of practice are subject to constant challenges that raise a range of emotions in the interviewer, and it is important to consider how these are best dealt with.
7. There is also consideration of when a matter requires the legal professional to consider onward referral to other qualified sources.

6.1 Finding the Pathway

No matter how hard we try to ensure that every interview achieves the outcomes that we are looking to achieve, the only guarantee that exists within legal client interviewing is that we cannot guarantee how any interview will proceed and what we will achieve.

DOI: 10.4324/9781003519096-6

The simple fact is that when you have any aspect of your life that involves a significant human aspect, then predictability and clear pathways that client and advisor merrily stroll along together are always going to be the exception rather than the rule.

Instead, it is all too easy to fall into a wide range of common situations where the interview leaves the track and heads to destinations new. These diversions can result from a wide range of sources sent to derail our aims. Often, the client can be the source of the issue with common problems resulting from the client who simply takes the interview as an opportunity to inform the advisor of a wide range of aspects of their life with only occasional tenuous links to the subject matter at hand. This can often then be contrasted with the client who wishes to divulge nothing except for what is directly enquired about – leading to an interview that lacks flow, direction, or personality.

Similarly, when the advisor is contently heading towards the crux of a legal issue, it can often be the case that the client becomes distracted or loses interest in the conversation, just at the point when you are seeking to make a point that is critical to your ongoing work together. Again, this can be contrasted with the client who is too engaged and takes the interview as an opportunity to unburden themselves via a level of truth and honesty that is more of an impediment than a help.

Finally, we also have to often deal with those familiar barriers to a smooth interview, namely conflict, aggression, distress, emotion, and the client who does not accept that you may be an expert in the law and who wishes to advise you on their own counsel regarding the matter at hand.

When introducing this segment, it would not be right and proper if consideration was not given to the way that legal advisors also often hijack their own process through interruption, the overwhelming need to hear their own voice, the use of technical language that obscures clarity, and in failing to maintain the distance required between the case at hand and the advisors need for professionalism. For example, a junior colleague (due to nerves during the interview) was unable to avoid a laugh escaping at the moment when the client reached the emotional highpoint of a challenging case.

Perhaps it is the very best part of what we do within the legal interview that these stumbling blocks exist as they show us the very human aspect of what we ask of our clients and what we ask of ourselves.

It is, therefore, important from the outset to never strive for the perfect interview – it rarely exists. Instead, we need to ensure that our efforts are designed around the creation of pathways that take us from our start through to our destination. These pathways will rarely be linear, they will twist, they will take turns, and they will occasionally head in the opposite direction to where we are aiming to reach, but as long as we know where the path needs to take us, then a few diversions along the way do not deter us – these diversions are in fact the way that we develop our skills and abilities to react to the adverse in a positive manner.

Within this chapter we will look to analyse some common issues within the interview and advice process with a view to providing a range of strategies to ensure that we get back to the path.

At the outset, we should start with two golden rules:

Rule 1 – A standard approach to interviews will not work with every client.
Rule 2 – People are people; embrace individuality.

6.2 Self-Reflection During the Interview

If the aim of the interview is to maintain proximity to the path between the two points of introduction and outcome, it is the most logical place to start with the aspects of the interview that we can control – namely ourselves.

As discussed in previous chapters, the role of the interviewer is to take the lead in directing the conversation. Taking the lead does not mean doing all of the talking and certainly does not require the legal professional to have a fixed destination in mind from the outset. They are a guide, and this role is vital in ensuring that the gathering of information is directed to the aim of providing accurate and appropriate advice.

Clients will follow the lead of the interviewer, so talking too quietly, too loudly, becoming distracted, looking bored, displaying emotion, etc., will provide the client with every opportunity to follow the lead given and to react in a similar fashion.

It is, therefore, incumbent upon the legal professional to adopt a position of ongoing reflection as part of the interview process.

The Solicitors Regulation Authority's guidance on continuing competence states that:

> Reflection is thinking about the challenges and quality of your practice so you can meet your competence requirements. These are to:
>
> - accurately evaluate your strengths and weaknesses in relation to the demands of your work, and
> - identify the learning and development needs you need to address to maintain your competence and provide high standards of service.

Reflective practice starts with the SRA's statement of solicitor competence, which lists the abilities and skills that constitute competence. To be able to reflect, we need to understand what we are reflecting about, and that commences with the competencies that we are required to demonstrate.

Section A2 of the competency statement requires that solicitors:

> Maintain the level of competence and legal knowledge needed to practise effectively, taking into account changes in their role and/or practice context and developments in the law, including:
> - taking responsibility for personal learning and development
> - reflecting on and learning from practice and learning from other people
> - accurately evaluating their strengths and limitations in relation to the demands of their work.

The process of completing reflective practice requires consideration of:

- What worked well?
- What went wrong and why?
- What needs to be done differently?
- What have I learnt?

However, within an interview format, it is vital that the process of reflection is not completed via some abstract reverie disconnected from the event. Instead, we are required to reflect and react within the moment as a means to ensure that we achieve the aim of information gathering with a view to providing appropriate advice.

This can be completed by tuning in to the responses of the client during the process. Subtle changes of approach can be key to ensure that the matter at hand moves back onto the required pathway.

So, if the climate of the interview does not feel correct, it is important to firstly check your own behaviour to ensure that the signals that you are providing are helping rather than hindering the process.

Consider whether you are demonstrating active listening, if your posture is open and you are radiating confidence, if you are encouraging responses, and if you are directing your questions to ensure that you can advise.

6.3 Content Issues

After consideration is given to the role that we are playing within the interview process, we then need to return to consideration of the aspects of an interview that are beyond our control – namely, the client side of the process. This requires us to understand how we can effectively manage and direct client interactions to address areas such as too much information, too little information, maintaining engagement, and client honesty.

6.3.1 Too Much Information

A very common occurrence within the client interview process is the client who will not stop talking. As a starting point, it is strange to have to consider this as a problem, as a client who provides us with no substantive information is clearly a bigger concern than a client who is providing us with significant amounts of detail in terms of outlining the matter at hand.

However harsh though it may seem, we do have to be commercially aware when we are holding initial meetings with clients. The average client interview schedule allows around 20 minutes with each new client. If we are therefore regularly taking more than double this allocation to gather the required information, then we are going to be taking forward far less clients and matters than our legal practice would require.

Even with the financial imperative ever in our thoughts, it can be a considerable challenge to arrest the client when they are in full flow and it is important to begin by understanding why the over talkative client is likely within the experience of every legal professional.

The first thing to consider is the important question of why a client will often seek to talk at length about their problem with someone that they may have just met for the very first time. It may seem strange, but it is largely a good thing to experience as the factors that have led to that moment must have achieved the purpose of ensuring that the client felt comfortable and confident to divulge the circumstances of their case, their situation, or their life in general.

Whilst our careful interview planning and process have started the client down the correct path, there may also be a number of other reasons behind the sudden deluge of information. Often, when we look at clients who are going through a divorce or a bankruptcy, the client's need to talk can often stem from a need to explain their side of the story with a view to releasing a sense of loss or injustice. In essence, the process of discussing the details of a case with someone can be cathartic – the notion of a legal advisor as a therapist.

This can make the idea of stepping in and curtailing the client's flow a source of guilt and can be counterproductive, as the client may feel that you do not wish to hear the case, and this builds barriers that can be difficult to then overcome. Similarly, it may be the situation that the client is talking because they do not feel that they are being heard. This often occurs where you may seem to be lacking attention.

There are also situations where the client is talking extensively around an issue as a means of avoiding discussing the issue at the very heart of their case.

If a client is, therefore, talking at length, it is important to have a series of techniques available to intervene and to recalibrate the conversation. One effective means of doing this is via the use of reflective statements.

Reflective statements are a highly effective way to curtail long statements but in a way that demonstrates empathy, understanding and shows that the client has been heard. The reflective statement can be particularly effective when it is followed by the use of a redirect immediately after.

An example of this would be:

> "I can see how much this has impacted upon you, and thank you for the detail that you have provided. Could you please tell me a little more about.?"

This will hopefully assist, but do not be afraid to be more direct if required. This could be:

> "Mrs White, I understand that this is a matter that has impacted upon you significantly in a number of differing ways. However, I note that our focus today is on the ongoing legal proceedings. Could you please concentrate initially on the background to the action?"

It is often beneficial to focus on not just the words that are used but also on the way that we can use body language with a view to getting the conversation back on track. This could include a subtle pointing with the pen, an opening of the mouth to suggest that you need to interject, or the use of a flat hand gesture to signify that the client can pause for a moment.

Eye contact can also be a valuable means to assert control within the interview. Where maintaining eye contact is a valuable tool in encouraging a client to continue, the breaking of eye contact can have the opposite effect. It is vital, of course, to do this whilst maintaining professionalism – so looking away towards notes may be appropriate, but gazing towards a clock would clearly be less so.

It should also be noted that whilst most interviews are enhanced through the utilisation of open questioning techniques, a client who continues to deviate from the path may need a more directed and, therefore, closed approach to questioning.

It is important to note that care does need to be taken, though. Often, it is easy to seek to curtail a conversation as you feel that you have the required level of understanding of the issue to move forward with advice. However, this builds assumptions into the process that can lead to a breakdown of the client relationship or could lead to the provision of incorrect or misleading advice.

6.3.2 Too Little Information

It can be frustrating to commence an interview with a client only to find that the client is stilted or uncommunicative in their interactions. Let's face it, they have arranged to see us, they have sought us out for our particular expertise, and we have devoted a finite amount of time and resources to helping this client to address the issue at hand. To then be left "pulling teeth" is often a real affront to our own position.

However, thought has to be given as to why clients often arrive at the interview and are reticent to engage. This starts with the basics of environment, whilst we are comfortable within our professional walls, it may well be the case that the client is crossing the threshold of a legal practice for the first time. The next consideration is the interview space itself, which can be too formal to encourage openness or too informal to maintain the view that the legal matter is being shared with a professional.

Our own appearance also has an effect: too formal and we can create a barrier (them and us); too casual and once again, we lose our shield of professionalism.

Consideration also has to be given to perhaps the key consideration – namely, that solicitors tend to be called upon when something has gone wrong. This could be a deeply personal criminal, family, or financial matter that may be difficult to discuss or may be embarrassing to the individual.

If a client is reserved at the outset, then it is very important to build effective rapport with a view to putting the client at ease. The use of tone and voice control can be key here as well as having an introduction that informs, sets the scene, and establishes credibility.

An example would be:

> "Hi, my name is Charlotte Sears, and I am a medical negligence solicitor here at Brown Bowden LLP. Today is just an opportunity for me to find out more about your case and to see how I might be able to help".

Once we get the client engaged in the conversation, it can often be the case that the issue of too little talking only comes to light as the appointment develops. This could be due to a variety of reasons, including content, non-verbal negative cues, verbal barriers, or issues with trust and confidence.

Should the client begin to close off the conversation during the interview, then it is possible that a question or observation has perhaps moved the client beyond their comfort zone.

It may also be the case that we have perhaps misjudged our own contribution to the conversation by perhaps introducing overly technical language, or we may have leapt ahead in our own thought processes without taking the opportunity to ensure that the client was with us.

At this point, the use of an explanation question can be helpful to get the matter back on track. This involves revisiting the subject matter from a softer position. An example would be:

> "Mr Haycock, I have asked you about the situation with your family because I do need to know what kind of financial support you will have in place should you decide to leave your partner. As we have already discussed, you are not in employment at this time and it may take some time until a financial settlement is agreed. Is there any support from family that you can all upon, until we can get this resolved?"

Of course, a legal professional should never shy away from considering a more direct approach where the situation warrants. The whole basis of the client/lawyer relationship is not designed around the idea of the client as a friend, and so we are often required to deliver bad news to those that we represent. Even during an initial meeting, a more direct approach can be a positive in reaffirming exactly why legal expertise and critical analysis are sought. An example would be:

> "Ms Zubair, I had thought that today's meeting was going quite well. However, I have noticed in the last few minutes that you have been more reluctant in your answers. Is there something wrong that we need to discuss?"

Another approach that can be used is to switch the style of questions from those that are more open and conversive to using a more closed and direct style to scaffold the client through more challenging content. An example would be:

> "Ms Gordon, we were talking about the moment you left the store and were stopped by security and asked to attend the security office with the guard. Did the guard restrain you physically? Was there a hand placed on your arm or your shoulder? Did you feel that the contact was inappropriate? Was anything further said to you as you were walked to the office? What was said?"

As well as the direct approach, a reflective stance can also assist:

> "Mr Paisley, we have been talking about the day that your husband informed you of his wish to leave the marital home. I am sure that this is upsetting to remember that day?"

Consideration should also be given to strategies that help to de-escalate challenging interview content. This involves placing the conversation into a more everyday, matter-of-fact context that can help the client to open up safely in the knowledge that they are not going to shock the advisor or perhaps create feelings of disapproval.

A reminder of our professional standards and expertise can assist:

> "Mrs Kendal, so it was after your husband had consumed alcohol that his behaviour changed. What particular behaviours frightened or upset you?"
>
> "I don't really like to talk about this. It was just terrible, but only after he had been at the pub".
>
> "Mrs Kendal, please do not worry about anything that we discuss today. I will not be shocked or surprised, and I can confirm that our conversations are entirely confidential. However, I do need to understand the specifics of his change of behaviour towards you".

Whilst many of the approaches outlined previously focus on verbal interactions, it is equally important to also ensure that we are aware of our non-verbal cues, as these can have either positive or negative outcomes on the client's confidence in interaction.

Using open, friendly postures, accompanied by a reduction in barriers (either physical or in our gestures), can assist. Whilst lingering eye contact can seem overbearing, regular eye contact and encouraging facial expressions help to show that you are interested and engaged with the client's story.

One specific area to consider is the temptation towards 'pen play'. This is where idle hands can often distract and inhibit the client, as the interviewer cannot resist spinning, clicking, or tapping the pen in their hands. This is often entirely subconscious but can require significant steps to avoid.

One approach that can assist in detecting distracting traits is to watch recorded interviews back with a focus on your own movements and how these impact upon the success of the meeting. This approach is facilitated by the expansion of online appointments via systems such as Zoom or Teams.

It should equally be noted that interview guides often state that those who cannot resist 'pen-play' would be best served by simply putting the offending item down to remove temptation. However, be wary as this can often signal that the interview is at an end, when the very opposite may be the case.

6.3.3 Client Engagement

Linked to the issue of clients finding it difficult to be open and conversive during the initial interview is the often-observed behaviour of a client who simply does not wish to listen. This may seem a strange topic – let's face it, the client will often have arranged the meeting with your legal practice and you would imagine that they would attend the meeting ready to engage and ready to listen to your sage words of legal advice.

However, it is often the case that the client attends the interview without actually being willing to take the advice that you wish to offer.

At this point, it is important to note that the legal professional is not there to insist upon a client's blind adherence to the pathway that the lawyer wishes them to follow. Instead, it is easier to think of solicitors as being more like taxi drivers. The client gets into the metaphoric back seat and tells us where to take them.

The wide scope of professional conduct areas that relate to the client relationship and matters of client care tells us that our role is to give the best advice that we can to a client; whether they choose to follow that advice or not does not materially change the way that we conduct our role.

Often, the starting point for a lawyer going 'unheard' can be traced back to events that occur before the meeting is even in the diary. Often a news story, a family experience, or the often quoted 'friend down the pub', instil in the mind of the client a fixed position of how the law relates to their specific matter. When we, as highly qualified legal advisors, then disrupt that view, the client will often seek recourse in their existing set of beliefs rather than accepting the expert's view.

In dealing with this, we simply go back to our cab – yes, we may know that the selected route is ill-advised, but it is the client's journey, and we are simply there to offer advice which may or may not be followed. Of course, our file management processes are best utilised by keeping a very detailed record in writing of what we suggested, should it become required to produce at a later point.

Another trigger for the client to wish to approach matters at a tangent to the strict legal advice occurs when the client is presented with an unexpected individual in the advisor's chair. This often happens when a client is used to dealing with a specific person, who may then be indisposed. Sadly, this also often occurs when the client is faced with an advisor who seems on the surface to lack experience or confidence in the matter at hand. This view can be based upon apparent age, gender, seniority, or any of a range of prejudices that the client may bring with them to the meeting.

The advised approach in dealing with this is to always focus on the areas that we can control. It is, therefore, important to return to the fundamentals of how we approach both the verbal and non-verbal aspects of the meeting. If we appear confident, then we are more likely to be accepted as the professional advisor in this matter. Confidence can be imbued from the feel of the initial handshake, the tone of voice used as the client is welcomed, the posture and gestures used in conveying the client to the meeting room, and the wording of questions and responses.

Whilst phrases such as "I think" will always suggest uncertainty, statements such as "I suggest" or "You have the following options", help to ensure that a level of assertiveness underpins the advisor's role.

Again, it is important that the legal professional is able to take the step of being direct and assertive with their client if they feel that the client's best interests are being clouded by a preconceived notion. This requires a delicacy of touch, but a firm but polite demonstration of your confidence can assist in directing a client back onto the path.

An example would be:

> "Daniel, it seems that we are heading in two different directions here. My advice is to follow the approach that I have outlined, and it seems that you are considering taking an opposing view. I sense that our different views may be linked to the fact that you do not have confidence in my skills and experience in this area. Please correct me if that is not the case. I appreciate that you are clearly more experienced with the running of the business. However, I am able to advise on more recent technological developments that are pertinent to the issue at hand. If we are able to work together, then we can find the ongoing solution that is needed here".

One thing to ensure is avoided at all costs, is to begin to take a defensive stance on the matter at hand. If a client fails to listen, you must always ask yourself, did you react as a professional to the circumstances presented? Not every client is going to hang on your every word, not every client is going to accept the offer that you have negotiated on their behalf, and not every client is going to choose to retain your services. These are beyond your control, and such outcomes should not lead to feelings of anger, defensiveness, or failure.

Instead, we focus on what is required of a professional, we give the best advice, we do the very best for every client, and we retain control of everything from when we contact the client when we advise certain steps, and we even maintain control when matters have not followed the plan by owning even the mistakes.

6.3.4 Client Honesty

A number of years ago, there was a substantial growth in claims related to illness experienced by holidaymakers. The nexus of the claims was a simple one. Members of the public booked to stay on an all-inclusive basis within a holiday resort hotel. They would, as is the nature of all-inclusive holidays, take their meals and drink their drinks at the hotel for the duration of their stay. It, therefore, followed that if the individual became unwell from matters related to food hygiene, then the case was made.

As with any area of law, clients were initially few and far between. However, awareness of the claims grew exponentially with every successful outcome until the number of claims was substantial.

However, this growth in awareness of the operation of sickness claims resulted in an increase in the possibility of claims that were dishonestly brought.

This dishonesty was possible to evidence as clients who had failed to tell the truth ultimately unmasked themselves. At the time, package holiday providers would ask returning travellers to complete a questionnaire on the flight home. One of the questions on the questionnaire related to general experience and another to the quality of food in the resort. It was amazing to see how many clients of legal firms had reported excellent holidays and high-quality food to then have commenced legal actions claiming a range of stomach-related illnesses.

Each and every one of those clients would have spoken with a legal professional, and it is highly likely that many told outright untruths to the solicitor to simply have their case taken on with a view to making financial gain.

It is not always easy, particularly when so many initial client interviews are conducted by telephone, to easily spot an untruth.

It is often only with experience that the legal interviewer gains a sixth sense or intuition as to when the story they are being told may be one of fiction rather than fact.

The main signs to identify, in a similar fashion to the previously-mentioned questionnaires, are when we start to see inconsistencies within the fact pattern of the case. This could be in the form of conflicting statements within an initial interview or could be in the form of variations within the story that become clear at a later point.

Further signs can be detected where the client exaggerates their description of events beyond the expected margins, as they wish to paint a positive view from their own perspective. It is also important to note that a failure to tell the whole truth does not always involve a specific statement; it is actually just as much of an issue where a client does not disclose the full story but instead edits the narrative for their own purposes.

If you suspect that a client is not being entirely upfront, consideration must be given as to why. If the matter is such that an outright untruth is being told to achieve gain, it is often difficult to refute this with certainty. However, the untruths are often a vehicle to avoid disclosing embarrassing information or details that would make the client appear foolish. It is also the case that the client may be trying very hard to ensure that you take forward their case and look to achieve the outcome that they wish to achieve – a non-malicious falsehood that is perhaps more a cry for help.

Where we detect that something seems very much amiss, a suggested approach is to provide an opportunity for reflection. This can be achieved by simply asking the client:

> "Is there anything that you would like to change in what you have just said? Sometimes, just thinking over something can help to ensure that I have all of the correct details".

An approach of this kind can often be successful in subtly letting the client know that something within their version of events does not add up. This tends to be advisable over the taking of a more direct approach, which can lead to great offence and irretrievably damage the client/lawyer relationship. Remember that however fanciful a story may seem, the history of law is littered with high-profile cases that, on the surface, would appear unlikely (snails and ginger beer bottles as an example). When in doubt, always err on the side of caution and remember, you were not there.

Another useful approach is to approach any inconsistencies on a point-by-point basis, addressing each issue in turn. There may be no attempt to deceive here, just a client who has mixed up key portions of the story. One way to do this is a simple,

> "Stuart, I am a little puzzled by a couple of things; could we just look at them again?"

Another approach is to put hypothetical propositions to the client that encourage them to see where the problem may be with their statement.

> "Mr Greenwood, you have mentioned today that you are not familiar with Mr Douglas, and yet we know that Mr Douglas has informed the police that you met in the pub to complete the exchange. The police are going to suggest that the reason you are denying knowing Mr Douglas is that you knew he was arriving with stolen goods. What would you say to that?"

In situations where the client is not revealing the whole truth, it may be required to point out to the client the consequences of proceeding with the current course of action, should it be based on an untruth.

The final point here is to mention the risks associated with representing someone who may be prone to hiding the truth. They are always going to be a difficult client to work with, and they can cause reputational issues for the legal professional as well. With that in mind, always consider that we are not required to represent those who come before us. We can always choose to walk away.

6.4 Mirroring

The non-verbal technique of mirroring has two facets that require consideration. Firstly, the use of the mirroring technique can be a significant positive in ensuring that clients are at ease in their conversations with the legal professional. In essence, the approach uses subtle variations in gesture, pacing, and tone to encourage the client to relax and engage effectively within the interview setting.

Effective use of gesture copying, mannerism adoption, and the utilisation of specific tones, speech patterns, and pace can be powerful influencers in building rapport with a client.

However, they do need to be used carefully, as mirroring, when too overt, can seem like you are mocking your client by mimicry. It is also possible for mirroring to be too successful as it can lead your client to mirror the interviewer and follow the interviewer's narrative rather than their own natural responses. This is particularly important if we are evaluating the reliability of a witness or where the client seems to be 'telling us what we want to hear'.

6.5 Client Issues

When it comes to client interviews, there is a wide range of different human factors that can occur, and all require clear planning to overcome.

6.5.1 Conflict and Aggression

Client aggression often occurs during the legal process due to feelings of being out of control and perhaps frustrated at delays, outcomes, or the behaviour of other parties. Often, it is the legal representative who bears the brunt of the client's bottled-up anger.

Dealing with aggressive clients requires great care with aggression encompassing a wide range of behaviours from passive forms through sarcasm, belittling comments, unreceptiveness, and impatience.

The approach to dealing with aggression often requires us to once again fall back upon our professional standards. Where it is easy to be drawn into personalising the client's approach towards you through negative responses, it is only through maintaining professional distance and through maintaining control of yourself and the situation that you will get matters back in hand.

Once again, it is what we do not say that begins to set the tone. The use of confrontational body language, eye contact, or gestures will typically serve to only inflame the situation. Instead, sitting confidently, the softening of expression, and a reduction in movement all aid the process of de-escalation.

Projecting calm also requires the use of our voice to exude calm and this can be achieved through the use of low, slow tones that maintain a professional pitch.

It is also useful to ensure that our responses have the effect of addressing the source of the aggression directly – seeming to deflect the issue can actually have a counterproductive effect.

"This is simply not good enough; I need to ensure that she is unable to do this to anyone else. The legal system should be here to support me. I have done nothing wrong here, and yet you are telling me that we cannot proceed to court to resolve this once and for all".

"Mr Clay, I appreciate your frustrations, and let us look at our options for response".

An awful lot of aggression from legal clients is actually a manifestation of the client wanting to be heard. It can, therefore, be a positive approach to simply allow the client to vent. This can be encouraged through the use of active and passive listening techniques which can often lead to the client's 'wind leaving the sails'.

Once the storm has passed, the client is then typically more malleable to listening as you tackle the issues raised on a point-by-point basis. This can be done in a calm and measured manner, with the client encouraged to accept the explanations as you systematically respond.

Perhaps one of the most challenging forms of aggression is the verbal attack that becomes personal and may even stray into the category of verbal abuse. It is advisable to simply not rise or respond to such conflict and instead return the focus to the issues at hand. A useful technique is to ask the client questions directed in this manner.

Of course, there may be circumstances where the client's ire is well founded and may, in fact, result from the legal practice itself, a rude welcome, a significant period of time kept waiting, a poorly timed intrusion, or a missed assignment can all result in client dissatisfaction. The approach is always to take responsibility, to ensure that an apology is provided and that actions are taken to respond positively to situations where an error has occurred.

Sources of aggression are usually best tackled by engaging directly with the behaviour with a view to understanding the client's position. Getting the client to talk can be very useful in uncovering the ongoing nature of many legal cases which are key in building our relationship and also our case.

Of course, there are limits to what can be seen as tolerable aggression, and it is important to ensure that legal practices operate as a team to support colleagues, to step in where client behaviour is inappropriate, and to ensure that safe systems of work are established via buddy systems, code alerts, or alarms that draw attention to ongoing violence or intimidation.

6.5.2 Client Distress

As legal advisors, we are rarely called upon to assist when a person's life is going incredibly well. Instead, we are there at what will often be the most difficult days of a person's life, and this can be during highly emotional times such as when someone has been dismissed from work, when a family break-up is underway, or when a family member has passed away.

Client distress can be underway before they even arrive at the legal practice or may start at any point during your interactions with them.

If this was your personal life, you would typically know how to deal with a specific individual in distress and would offer comfort, a reassuring hand, or even an embrace. Of course, clients are rarely people that we know on that level of understanding, and so responses are challenging when we are faced with a sudden breakdown of composure.

The only thing you can usually guarantee is that it would be a rare legal career not to have to face a client in an emotional state.

The first thing to say is that you cannot simply ignore what is happening in front of you. Yes, they are a client, and we are not going to be offering a hug of condolence, but we cannot simply freeze as if the situation is not taking place. Instead, it is better to use our skills of empathy and understanding to assist the client at these moments.

One such approach is to state:

> "Ashab, I am really sorry that we are having to discuss something which is clearly upsetting to go over. Take your time, and when you are ready, we can take this one step at a time. Would you like to have a break for a few minutes?"

Once again, we can also look to move away from our open question style to a more directed series of closed questions. These could be as follows:

> "Ashab, let us take our time and just go one step at a time. When did she return to the family home? And she stayed there for how many days? At what point did

> she become violent towards you? Did this require medical attention? What were the injuries?"

An alternative approach is to move the conversation away from the point of distress to a more prosaic subject.

> "Ashab, there are more things that we need to look at here, but let's leave them for now, and we can look at them at a later date. For the moment, can I ask you about.?"

When a matter is such that the client is unable to express what is required within the formality of an interview, it can be a useful suggestion to ask the client to write down the information in their own time and then share this with you either via correspondence or within the next meeting. This serves to reduce the pressure whilst still ensuring that you have the information required to proceed.

6.5.3 Dealing With Self-Emotion

Many positive aspects flow from the ability to engage with the client on the appropriate level, and this can be a vital aspect of building trust, confidence, and the foundations of a working relationship.

However, it is possible to be so attuned with the client that you can start to lose that all-important critical distance, and this can be inadvertently displayed particularly in moments of high emotion.

Tension, embarrassment, anxiety, or nervous traits can be easily displayed without the legal professional even knowing that they are in the process of manifestation. Suddenly, there is a subconscious change in expression, tone, posture, or vocabulary, and this can be a real challenge to the ongoing professional relationship as it can be viewed as either 'a mask slipping' or becoming too close to the client to remain objective.

Of course, by the time you are aware that you have succumbed to emotional contagion, you are largely past the point where any positive actions can be taken to recover the situation beyond empathy and the hope that the event does not materially undermine the ongoing process of working collaboratively with your client.

The main approaches that can be taken in this regard are around ongoing personal development. Once you have allowed the client to see behind Oz's curtain, you are actually much better prepared to identify the signs of any future event.

It takes a lot of self-awareness to be able to spot when someone else's emotions are making you emotional, too, and over time, you will find that understanding how to control your emotions can actually make it far easier to address the situation without acting upon the emotional core.

For highly emotional situations, the use of active and passive listening provides an opportunity for you to break the emotional build-up through momentary interjections that allow a moment for you to recover your previous professional passivity.

6.5.4 Referral

It may seem harsh to consider, but if we are able to put into practice many of the techniques of empathy, listening, encouragement, and support in our work as legal professionals, we may have to face the result that the client is too willing to open up to us. This can be problematic when we consider that whilst we may be considered as a confidant, advisor, guide or even friend to our clients, our clients should remain as clients and nothing more.

It is, therefore, important to always plan ahead and have a good awareness of alternative support provision that exists within a client's local area. One particular example of this comes about where a client displays all of the symptoms of stress disorders, or anxiety, related to a matter pertinent to their case. Where this occurs, it is often experienced that the client will seek to use the legal professional as a form of counsellor. This is something that must be managed as no matter how much you may wish to help, you are not qualified to assist with matters beyond your expertise, and this is also not good for business as you are paid to resolve legal matters and not personal problems – no matter how closely related the two things may be.

With this in mind, ensuring that you keep up to date with a wide range of financial, personal, health, and support services within your area allows you to provide the very best service to your clients by ensuring that they can be referred to specialist and professional assistance.

However, it can be difficult to broach the subject of onward referral with a client who has closely aligned themselves with you. The first point here is to ensure that you take steps at the earliest opportunity to consider onwards recommendation as this will have the effect of maintaining parameters, something that proves much more difficult at a later stage when positions are more entrenched.

It is also important to ensure that the client feels that any suggestion of referral is coming from the right place and is not approached as a topic that could be considered as pushing the client away. One approach that can work here is to ensure that the client has full support from you in accessing ongoing assistance. This could even involve offering to make arrangements, but it will be situation-specific.

In Summary

Maintaining Effective and Professional Relationships with Clients

A competent legal professional will be able to:

- Allow the client to make decisions by providing them with all the relevant information and evidence, including complaint processes.
- Build a relationship of trust with the client by addressing their concerns and responding sensitively to their needs.
- Be respectful to all clients and act in a way that promotes equality, diversity, and inclusion.
- Identify when a client may be regarded as vulnerable and ensure provisions are made available to the client to fully access legal services both before instruction and after.
- Provide advice and guidance that is tailored in language and style according to the client's emotional, physical, neurodiverse, cultural, or other needs.
- Handle sensitive situations as they arise by diffusing tensions, offering comfort and empathy where needed, and avoiding patronising the client.

Interviewing and advising

A competent legal professional will be able to:

- Prepare for an interview
- Allow clients or professional advisers to explain their concerns
- Identify the client's goals and priorities
- Use appropriate questioning techniques
- Determine what further information is required
- Identify possible courses of action and their consequences
- Establish a professional relationship with the client and deal with any ethical problems that may arise

Ethics, Professionalism, and Judgement

A competent legal professional will be able to:

- Recognise ethical issues and exercise effective judgement in addressing them
- Understand and apply the ethical concepts which govern their role and behaviour as a lawyer
- Identify the relevant SRA principles and rules of professional conduct and follow them
- Resist pressure to condone, ignore or commit unethical behaviour
- Respect diversity and act fairly and inclusively

Key Practice Case

The case of *Solicitors Regulation Authority Ltd v Sunny Sidhu* (2024) SDT 12523–2023 is a reminder of the need for lawyers to maintain the highest professional standards when dealing with vulnerable clients.

In the case, Mr Sidhu, whilst employed at LDJ Solicitors, was instructed to advise the client in respect of her divorce proceedings with a view to obtaining a prohibited steps order against the father of her children.

Utilising his position, Mr Sidhu contacted the claimant stating that he required a series of explicit images from the client with a view to protecting her from a possible act of revenge porn, which it was suggested that her ex-husband might perpetrate.

During the hearing before the Solicitors' Disciplinary Tribunal, Sidhu accepted that he had known that the client was vulnerable, although he maintained that the images had not been obtained for his own personal gratification.

However, the tribunal found that:

> For the next six weeks [Sidhu] requested the explicit photos and videos in every conversation that they had and would reiterate what he said in their first conversation regarding revenge porn. He also emphasised that revenge porn would be her ex-husband's next move and that there would be nothing he could do to help her if he did not already have the photos.

Sidhu informed the client that the photos would be uploaded to a confidential file on a secure system within the firm and deleted from a mobile phone that was used to enable the image transfer. However, Sidhu did not disclose at any point that the telephone in question was his personal number.

The solicitor was found to be dishonest, and his conduct was "clearly inappropriate" and was "clearly sexually motivated". The tribunal concluded that:

> There was no credible motivation for the respondent to request explicit images from Person A other than in pursuit of sexual gratification or in pursuit of a future sexual relationship.
>
> [Sidhu] used his position as a solicitor to request and receive these images, which was an abuse of his position. Person A trusted the respondent at a time when she was vulnerable and felt incapable of making decisions for herself; the respondent knew or ought to have known this.

> The public would be appalled at [Sidhu's] behaviour, engineering a situation in which he could request explicit images from a client and then pestering her, through his position of authority as a solicitor, to send them to his personal mobile phone.

The solicitor was struck off, and he was ordered to pay costs of £32,394.72.

The case serves as an example of the importance of appropriate conduct in dealing with vulnerable clients.

Practice Tips

- Apply common sense to everyday situations and ensure that client care and professional conduct rules remain at the forefront of your mind when dealing with the client.
- Remember that the relationship with a client is one that only truly operates where trust and confidence exist.
- Always ensure that critical distance is employed within client interactions with a view to maintaining professional balance within the confines of the conduct rules.
- Each client interaction will be unique, and you will be required to demonstrate mental agility, flexibility, and skills of adaptation in the way that you handle cases at the initial interview and advice stage, particularly in highly emotional circumstances, interactions where anger is present, or where the client is vulnerable.

Practice Risks

- Any of the previous issues can lead to situations where the client does not provide the legal advisor with adequate detail to allow for an effective review of the matter at hand.
- A failure on the part of the legal advisor to correctly handle conflict situations during the interview could easily lead to the loss of a client and reputational damage.
- Failure to apply the professional rules and codes of conduct correctly.
- The potential for the interview process to be a means of exacting control over a client in terms of the case and potentially in wider aspects of their life.
- Failure to seek guidance from senior colleagues or the professional body when an interview has gone awry.

Exercises

EXERCISE A

Read the three examples which follow and

Say whether the interviewer's response is satisfactory and, if not,
How could the interviewer's responses could be improved?

Example 1

Interviewer: Mrs Gordon, you mentioned earlier that you had experienced some strange behaviour from your work colleagues.

Mrs Gordon: Yes. After the accident happened, I was in contact with work friends for the first couple of weeks; this might have been a call or a message on our chat group or to me directly. However, since then, I have heard nothing at all from them, and I don't know why.

Interviewer: That is unusual, and I can see why that would be upsetting.

Mrs Gordon: It has been. Working in a small office, we have always been friendly, and that applies to not just the staff but the managers as well. However, since this whole process started, it seems that they are ignoring me. Last week, I saw my colleague Lisa in town. I am sure that she saw me, and yet she simply crossed over the road and walked on as if she had not seen me. That's after we have been colleagues for over five years. We have even been out socially on a number of occasions. I am now even worried about trying to reach out to them.

Interviewer: Have you tried getting in contact with any of them recently? Is there perhaps one specific person you could contact? This might be a good way to know, once and for all, if they really are ignoring you.

Mrs Gordon: I suppose that I could try contacting Alicia.

Example 2

Interviewer: Mrs Gordon, you mentioned earlier that you had experienced some strange behaviour from your work colleagues.

Mrs Gordon: Yes. After the accident happened, I was in contact with work friends for the first couple of weeks; this might have been a call or a message on our chat group or to me directly. However, since then, I have heard nothing at all from them, and I don't know why.

Interviewer: It's probably nothing. At this stage of the process, your employer is now aware that you have brought a claim against them, so your friends may have been told not to talk to you.

Mrs Gordon: (Upset) But we are friends, and they shouldn't be able to tell us that we cannot speak to each other.

Interviewer: (Stands up) Look, I'll get you a glass of water. Then, we can get back to the case.

Example 3

Mrs Gordon: After the accident happened, I was in contact with work friends for the first couple of weeks; this might have been a call or a message on our chat group or to me directly. However, since then, I have heard nothing at all from them, and I don't know why.

Interviewer: Yes, that must be very upsetting. Now, returning to the day of the accident. When exactly did you report it to the company?

The previous examples are not designed to provide a specific guide to what should be said or not said when faced with a situation where a client wishes to discuss the impact of an accident in terms of their established relationships with colleagues. Instead, they are designed to provide a range of responses that are all too often what will be heard during an interview where the client wishes to discuss a wide range of matters, whilst the interviewer is simply seeking to direct the conversation to what is required for the matter at hand.

When looking at the responses, it may be the case that you can relate the interviewer's response to your own experience, and it may, therefore, be that your feelings regarding the merits of each example.

EXERCISE B

Read the example which follows, and

- Consider the types of questions that the interviewer uses during the passage.
- Analyse how the question impacts upon the interaction with the client
- Evaluate whether the question could have been improved.
- Suggest how the questions could have been approached.

Interviewer: Hello, is it Mrs Gordon?

Mrs Gordon: Hello, yes

Interviewer: Hi, Mrs Gordon. My name is Terry Cokell, and I am one of the legal team here at Bowden, Bowden, and Bowden Solicitors. Please come in and take a seat.

Mrs Gordon: Thank you.

Interviewer: How can I help?

Mrs Gordon: I'm not actually sure where to start.

Interviewer: Well, I note from your enquiry that you have had an accident at work. Is that right?

Mrs Gordon: Yes, that's right.

Interviewer: Well, let's start from there. Could you start by telling me a little about the type of work that you do?

Mrs Gordon: Well, I' ve not been able to work at all since I had my accident.

Interviewer: I see, and I am sorry to hear that. Could you please advise me as to what your job role was before the accident?

Mrs Gordon: I was an administrator for the local council.

Interviewer: Had you worked for the council for long?

Mrs Gordon: I started back in 2016, so around seven or eight years.

Interviewer: Thanks for that. Now, could you tell me a little about the accident itself?

Mrs Gordon: Where would you like me to start?

Interviewer: Let's start with the basics and go from there. So firstly, when exactly did it happen?

Mrs Gordon: The accident happened back in December 2023.

Interviewer: Thank you. Now, can you tell me exactly what happened?

Mrs Gordon: The accident happened when I was asked to help to move a large amount of photocopying that had been sent to our office. The documents were required by our events team and had been sent to us in error. However, we needed the space clearing, and it would have taken too long to get the facilities team across to move them. So, we all pitched in.

Interviewer: So, just to confirm, it is not a normal part of your duties to move boxes of paper?

Mrs Gordon: Absolutely not. My role tends to involve data entry, but as a team, we were looking to pitch in and help.

Interviewer: Not everyone had an accident, though, did they?

Self-Reflection Checklist

What three important things have you learnt from this chapter?	**1**	**2**	**3**
Set out the three additional steps that you need to take to learn the skills in this chapter in more detail.	**1**	**2**	**3**

7 The SQE2 Client Interview

Key Chapter Points

1. This chapter provides the reader with a step-by-step guide to effective preparation and completion of the SQE2 Interviewing assessment.
2. The process of completing the SQE Interviewing Assessment is one that presents a real challenge to the candidate as information is only released during the session, and the client is an SQE assessor trained in testing a candidate's capability in an interview setting.
3. To be considered a competent legal interviewer, it is important that the candidate is able to conduct the appointment to the expected standards as set out by professional bodies and associated codes.
4. From the preparation to be completed before the assessment day, through the initial 10-minute preparation period, and onwards through the appointment itself, the chapter provides guidance and advice on how to achieve when under pressure.
5. The chapter also looks to provide the interviewer with a structured approach, from building initial rapport through effective questioning and legal advice to the requirement to provide appropriate options and ending with client care.
6. The chapter culminates with two fully worked examples that focus on the assessment areas of property practice and wills and the administration of estates.

7.1 Introduction

When it comes to the skills of client interviewing and legal analysis, this text has been prepared to provide the reader with the opportunity to develop their skills, knowledge, and a series of strategies for successful interactions within the legal setting.

However, it would be remiss if we did not take a specific look at the requirements placed upon those who are seeking to be successful in their SQE2 Client Interviewing and Completion of Attendance Note/Legal Analysis assessments.

DOI: 10.4324/9781003519096-7

7.2 The SQE2 Interviewing Assessment

The SQE2 Client Interviewing and Completion of Attendance Note/Legal Analysis assessment is divided into two distinct parts.

The first segment requires the student to successfully complete a client interview, whilst the second component requires that the student drafts a full attendance note.

To date, this text has focused on the first of these, with consideration of legal analysis and attendance notes, as follows in Chapter 8. The assessment itself is, therefore, unusual as it requires a candidate to demonstrate both oral and written skills within the same task.

In analysing the assessment, we will look at:

- The process
- The assessment criteria that apply
- How to effectively prepare for the assessment
- How to use the 10-minute preparation period most effectively
- The role of the client in the assessment
- The advised structure for the interview
- The requirement for effective relationship-building
- Conduct and ethics
- The requirement (potentially) to negotiate
- Advice on the taking of notes
- Time

7.3 The Process

The SQE2 assessment for Client Interviewing and Completion of Attendance Note/Legal Analysis is a critical station which is designed to assess your ability to engage effectively with clients, to elicit information, to provide sound advice, and to develop an appropriate action plan.

The assessment takes the form of role-play, with the candidate required to take on the role of the legal professional, with a trained assessor taking on the role of the client. The test seeks to recreate the skill of conducting a legal interview – a critical skill for the day one solicitor.

It is important to note that candidates will actually be required to complete two interviews as part of their SQE2 assessment in this area. The first interview will be based within the area of property law and practice, and the second, conducted on the following day, requires the student to complete an interview with a client seeking advice on topics within the area of wills, intestacy, probate, and the administration of estates.

It is important to note that students are not specifically being tested on their knowledge of these areas of the law (these are, after all, two elements of the functioning legal knowledge that is assessed within SQE1. However, any effective interview is going to require a student to have a suitable understanding of the law if they are to prepare questions and advise appropriately.

As well as having a working knowledge of the underlying black letter law, students are also advised that the assessment *may* involve elements of negotiation and will require students to demonstrate an understanding of relevant ethical and professional conduct issues.

The first step in the process will be the provision of an e-mail from a partner or a secretary stating the basic details of the client and the matter.

The SRA website provides an example of what a candidate will receive. Two alternative sets of instructions are provided in the exercises and are available later in this chapter.

Upon receipt of the e-mail, you are then provided with 10 minutes in which you can prepare the specific areas that you are going to approach during the assessment.

It should be noted that you are provided with 25 minutes in which to conduct the interview and then given a further 25 minutes in which to write up the attendance note.

7.4 Assessment Criteria

In the SQE2 Client Interviewing and Completion of Attendance Note/Legal Analysis assessment, candidates are assessed against a range of different criteria.

In terms of the interviewing component, candidates are required to 'demonstrate they are able to conduct an interview with a client'.

This requires students to demonstrate their competence against five skills criteria:

1. Listen to the client and use questioning effectively to enable the client to tell the solicitor what is important to them.
2. Communicate and explain in a way that is suitable for the client to understand.
3. Conduct themselves in a professional manner and treat the client with courtesy, respect, and politeness, including respecting diversity where relevant.

4. Demonstrate client-focus in their approach to the client and the issues (i.e., demonstrate an understanding of the problem from the client's point of view and what the client wants to achieve, not just from a legal perspective).
5. Establish and maintain an effective relationship with the client so as to build trust and confidence.

For the attendance note/legal analysis aspect of the process, candidates are required to demonstrate their competence by producing 'an attendance note recording a client interview and initial legal analysis'.

The skills criteria that candidates are assessed against are:

1. Record all relevant information.
2. Identify appropriate next steps.
3. Provide client-focused advice (i.e., advice which demonstrates an understanding of the problem from the client's point of view and what the client wants to achieve, not just from a legal perspective).

In addition, students are also assessed on their application of the law, as follows:

4. Apply the law correctly to the client's situation.
5. Apply the law comprehensively to the client's situation, identifying any ethical and professional conduct issues and exercising judgment to resolve them honestly and with integrity.

A full breakdown of the performance indicators for a client SQE2 Interview assessment can be found by visiting the SRA website at:

https://sqe.sra.org.uk/docs/default-source/pdfs/sqe2-sample-questions/int-performance-indicators.pdf?sfvrsn=69961d98_2

Similarly, the performance indicators for the attendance note/legal analysis component can be found by visiting the following link:

https://sqe.sra.org.uk/docs/default-source/pdfs/sqe2-sample-questions/an-performance-indicators.pdf?sfvrsn=bb25fac0_1

7.5 Preparing for Assessment

It is a well-used adage to say that failure to prepare is simply preparing to fail, and that is certainly true of any aspect of the assessment process for SQE1 or 2. The whole nature of both multiple-choice assessments and skills-based activities is one where what we do in the days, weeks, and months before will have a significant impact on what we achieve on the day.

It is therefore important for us to look at how candidates can use the time prior to assessment day as effectively as possible and also how that 10-minute preparation period can best be utilised to drive success.

7.5.1 Pre-Assessment Day

The starting point for preparing for assessment day is to ensure that you are familiar with the law that is to be the basis of your oral assessments. As mentioned previously, the day one interview will be about property law and practice, and the following day, we will need to be prepared with our knowledge of wills, intestacy, probate, and administration of estates.

As you may be aware, these are both technical areas of law that require specific knowledge of law, process, and requirements.

It is important to note that whilst it is true to say that you are not going to lose marks for a failure of knowledge in these areas of law – your knowledge is assessed within SQE1 – it is almost impossible to ask questions of a client if you are unaware of what you need to ask about.

It will also be ill-advised to fail to prepare adequately, as without the correct knowledge, you may be unable to complete either the advice stage of the interview or the application of the law within the attendance note.

Of course, whilst the law is clearly an important aspect of preparation, it would be incorrect to approach the assessment with simply the law and nothing further. A student who knows the law but is unable to interview a client adequately would be deemed not yet competent in an assessment that is seeking to test whether you have the skills of a 'day one solicitor'.

It is, therefore, essential to ensure that time is spent and opportunities are taken to practice the skills of interviewing as you approach the assessment date. It is important to note that just knowing the interview process will likely be insufficient, as it is only by taking as many opportunities as you can that you develop that required approach to legal interviewing, where it appears to be second nature.

It is often said that there is no perfect solicitor, but there is a solicitor who can draw upon multiple experiences, and interviewing is very much one of those areas where the more you do, the easier the process becomes.

As a piece of practical advice, by accessing the sample assessment – which can be viewed using the following link – https://sqe.sra.org.uk/docs/default-source/pdfs/sqe2-sample-questions/sqe2-sample-question-interview-attendance–2023.pdf?sfvrsn=ea49b6e7_1 – you can work with a friend, colleague, fellow student or family member to practise elements of the interview.

As an example, it should be relatively straightforward to move from a planned and scripted introduction to an introduction that requires no notes, no reading, and can simply be stated with confidence within a relatively short space of time. Once this is achieved, then it is knowledge that will not require further consideration – it has become automatic.

Another area which can be helpful to practice is how to explain legal concepts in a manner that can be easily understood by a lay person. This is where family and friends who are not legally qualified can be particularly useful. If you can explain intestacy to a person who has not studied this area, then you are well on your way to being able to advise on this technical area during the assessment.

Of course, within the subjects of Property Law and Wills and Probate, there are significant areas that could form part of the assessment. With this in mind, consider alternative scenarios that may be used within the assessment itself. This could, for example, be the purchase of a house, the law regarding adverse possession, or regarding leasehold or freehold rights. Similarly, you could be looking at a matter of intestacy, the validity of a will, or whether provisions could be raised within the Inheritance (Provision for Family Dependants) Act 1975.

It is vital that you take the time to brush up on these areas to ensure that you understand the relevant tests that would apply in each area. By knowing these tests, we can then reverse engineer the process of creating questions that would be relevant during the interview.

For example, intestacy requires that there is no valid will in existence. The relevant question would, therefore, be to ask if there was a will.

7.5.2 Effective Use of the 10-Minute Preparation Period

As highlighted previously, the assessment starts with the assessor handing a set of instructions to the candidate, and you are provided with a 10-minute period in which to prepare. It is important to note that 10 minutes is clearly a very short window in which to adequately prepare for the interview, particularly now that the facts are known. It is, therefore, essential that you have a clear plan in place to ensure that you use the time available effectively.

The first step is to ensure that you read the instructions provided carefully, mentally highlighting key requirements and also any areas that do not require consideration.

Areas to focus on include:

- The client's name
- The area of law under consideration

- Whether costs need to be discussed – it may be the case that the instructions specifically tell you that this area does not require coverage. If this does happen, note this, as there is nothing to gain by wasting your 25 minutes discussing topics that gain no marks.
- Similarly, client care may also be specifically excluded and should be noted.

It can be helpful to highlight or underline key information as you read the instructions to ensure that you focus on the key information. This also saves time searching back for areas that you need to consider.

When it comes to the assessment, there is no set rule as to how much content you may be provided with. This could be a detailed example or it could be as simple as an instruction that your client is coming to see you for advice on the process of purchasing a house.

Regardless of the details provided, you should be able to quickly identify the key information, based on your pre-assessment preparation, that you will need to request from the client. However, it is important to remember that this is a client interview assessment and not an assessment of your ability to talk about an area of law. With this in mind, be careful not to prejudge the matter and to ensure that you retain an open-mind with a view to ensuring that you format your interview as a means to gather information from the client rather than putting words in the client's mouth.

If we do not hear the story from the client, we are in danger of making assumptions that can lead to information being missed and advice being off-point.

One useful approach is to develop a list approach to structuring the interview. In essence, a decision tree approach where the answer to one question then allows the interview to be led into the next consideration.

As well as the e-mail, it is also possible for the assessment to feature a document that is part of the client's matter. Again, this should be viewed carefully, with segments highlighted or underlined and notes taken that form the basis of the approach to questioning.

As an example, in the second interview, you may be presented with a will. The approach here should be to ensure that you are familiar with the provisions and clauses within the document. However, always be aware of the more basic areas of knowledge – such as considerations of validity or gift failure.

It is also important to note any additional information you have that underpins the appointment itself. It may be the case that the instructions give considerable detail about the nature of the enquiry, or it may be the very opposite.

With the approach considered, it is also important to ensure that you have sufficient materials to aid the making of contemporaneous notes. Make sure that you have checked pens are working, pencils are sharpened, highlighters are sufficient, and that you have suitable paper to record the details gleaned during the discussion.

It is a helpful approach to actually set out your notes with headings that will help you prepare your attendance notes as part of the 10-minute period. This allows you to slot information into your notes quickly but will also help to guide your questioning whilst also making the attendance note-writing aspect of the task a simpler process.

7.6 The SQE2 Client

Whilst it is the case that the interview will be a role play between a candidate and an assessor, it should not be overlooked that the assessment process has been designed to be as authentic an experience as possible.

The assessment team employed to complete the interview assessments are experienced in ensuring that the approach taken will ensure that the client is portrayed in a manner that is as real-life as possible. This means that the client may well be that ideal client who is polite, reasonable, practical, prepared, and helpful, but it is equally possible that they will be the very opposite and may place a number of obstacles in the candidate's path, which could include, interruption, a failure to communicate effectively, or even an unwillingness to accept the advice offered.

Whilst this may seem unfair, it is important that successful candidates are equally adept at dealing with perfect clients as they are those who present more difficulties if they are to demonstrate competence.

It is, therefore, important to use the guidance provided in this text to ensure that you can deal with any situation that may be present on the day. As an example, if you are dealing with a client who tends to provide long-winded answers to open questions, it may be helpful to use some closed questioning techniques as a means to shorten responses and to allow you to focus on the case at hand.

It is also important to ensure that your approach to your client is within the expectations of a legal professional. As an example, if you are faced with a client who has recently suffered a bereavement, it would be incorrect to fail to empathise with the client's situation just because the client is an assessor playing a role.

A key consideration is the ability to flexibly deliver advice to this specific client, rather than relying upon general approaches. As an example, if you are dealing with a client where English is not a first language, you may need to consider approaches to ensure that written advice is appropriate.

Such issues may be immediately apparent during the appointment, but it is rarely advisable to assume. With this in mind, candidates are encouraged to consider the use of a set accessibility statement as part of the interview introduction.

An example would be:

> "Please let me know if there is anything that I can do to ensure that my advice is accessible as possible or if you have any preferences to how we communicate with you".

7.7 Generic Interview Structures for Assessment

Whilst we have spent considerable time within this text looking at how to conduct a professional legal interview, it is important that we now take the opportunity to summarise how to approach an interview when it is being assessed.

The following is a suggested structure that could be considered as a suitable approach for the interview assessment. It should be noted that these are suggested segments of the interview and, as such, can be varied, amended, or added to as required to ensure that the interview is as comfortable for the candidate as possible.

7.7.1 Greeting the Client

It is important to note that the assessment criteria provided by the SRA states that a candidate should:

> Conduct themselves in a professional manner and treat the client with courtesy, respect and politeness including respecting diversity where relevant.

The SRA performance indicators confirm that to be assessed as competent, an individual must:

- Treat the client with courtesy and respect
- Behave politely and build rapport with the client

Like with a driving test where the learner is able to pull away from the test centre in a confident and assured manner, it is important that the interview commences on the right foot from the very start.

For this reason, the importance of a suitable, warm, professional, and friendly greeting cannot be over-emphasised. If this is completed successfully, a nervous client can be made to feel comfortable, relaxed, and engaged with the interview itself. If this step is missed or is dealt with badly, then the examiner will already be forming a view that the candidate is not yet ready to be released upon the legal world.

As with all communication, there are two key considerations – what is said and how we say it.

When it comes to the words themselves, it tends to be advisable to commence the interview with a simple approach that can be easily delivered in as natural a manner as possible.

The introduction should include your name, your company, and details or your role.

An example would be:

> "Good afternoon, Mrs White. My name is Kimberley Barker, and I am a Solicitor here at ABC Law. It's a pleasure to meet you".

In addition, it is important to ensure that non-verbal communication is managed effectively. This should include suitable eye-contact and open but not distracting mannerisms.

As a next step, it is always advisable to ensure that the client is at ease through the use of everyday conversation that does not immediately focus on the legal issue at hand. This is particularly important as the process of engaging a legal professional is not, for the vast majority of members of the public, an everyday occurrence and is, therefore, likely to give rise to some anxiety. When it is considered that the requirement to contact a solicitor is often aligned with a difficult period in someone's life, we can see that some level of normality in the interview conversation can be of great assistance.

Within the SQE2 assessment, it can therefore be advisable to ensure that you have a range of topics in mind that can be used at this initial stage. These could include anything from the weather to a recent positive news story or could be about the client's journey to the appointment.

It should be noted that whilst these areas can provide a useful means to ease the initial stages of the interview process, they must be something that you can put across in as genuine a manner as possible. Should the attempt at friendly conversation seem scripted or forced, then it can have the opposite effect of actually reducing the establishment of rapport.

Added challenges result from the expansion in the use of virtual interviews, which can severely inhibit the opportunities to build rapport whilst also heightening a client's sense of anxiety. In these circumstances, the approach and advice do not change; in fact, it may be more important than ever to ensure that you work to build rapport.

Of course, with introductions completed, it is then important to ensure that the interview assessment progresses to the following stages: the interview has a 25-minute timeframe, and hence, it is vital to complete the initial stages and then move forward.

7.7.2 Preliminary Points

With the pleasantries covered, it is important for the legal professional to ensure that the client is aware of a range of information at the start of the interview. By completing this correctly, the interview can be started on the correct footing, and a number of questions can be saved at a later stage, saving both time and confusion.

With a greeting and confirmation of your role confirmed in the initial introduction, the legal professional can then move to cover a range of topics, including the basis of the initial interview, the position regarding confidentiality, how the interview will be structured, and even areas such as the taking of notes and discussions regarding fees and funding.

This stage is always a good opportunity to ensure that details about the matter are also clarified. It is often the case that you will attend an interview with very brief details, and you will need to have much greater detail before you can even look at the approach you may take to the appointment.

As an example, 'I want to see a solicitor about a housing matter' could mean a conveyance, a tenancy agreement, an eviction, a neighbour dispute, or a transfer between joint tenants to tenants in common. Due to this, it is always good to ask a starting question that clarifies the nature of the enquiry, but care does need to be taken to ensure that the client does not see this as an opportunity to go into the minutiae of the case facts. Using a closed question, can assist, such as:

> "You have mentioned that this is a housing matter. Could you please briefly clarify the issue?"

In some circumstances, this could actually bring the interview to an end – if the enquiry is perhaps outside of the firm's services or expertise, saving considerable time and effort.

However, as with the SQE assessment itself, we will assume that the matter is within our experience, and we can, therefore, look at how best to ensure that we open the conversation in an appropriate fashion.

- **The basis for the appointment**
  It is often the case that the client's initial anxiety in speaking with a solicitor is the fear that the charging of fees is already underway. It is possible at times to

see clients concerned that they have perhaps hailed a particularly expensive taxi and the meter is running. It is for this reason that many firms offer a free initial consultation to clients, and it is important to ensure that this is communicated to the client at the earliest opportunity to ensure that the conversation that follows is one where both parties are relaxed and open.

This can be confirmed by advising the client that "today's appointment is provided under the firm's free advice service, and so there is no charge for this initial meeting".

Simple confirmation is often all that a client needs to set a positive opening.

It is important to note that paragraph 8.7 of the Code of Conduct requires that legal professionals ensure that the client is given the best information possible at the time of engagement and as the matter progresses.

- **Confidentiality**

  As mentioned previously, it is rarely the case that a client engages a solicitor due to life going very well. Instead, it is often at the lowest moments that a solicitor enters the fray. By their very nature, challenging moments in a person's life tend to be the sort of details that the client would rather not share too widely, be that discussing marital issues, the death of a loved one, or criminality.

  It can, therefore, be beneficial to use the preliminary segment of the session to ensure that the client is aware that any information provided will be dealt with in a confidential manner. This can also be a good opportunity to affirm the trust that they can place in you as a result of the relevant duty within the code of conduct.

  This could be approached as follows:

  > "I do wish to confirm that anything that we discuss today will be dealt with confidentially. In fact, we have a duty of confidentiality to all clients that covers anything we are told and even any notes that we take during the interview".

- **The structure of the interview**

  It is good practice for both the SQE2 assessment and for work in practice to ensure that clients are aware of how the interview will be conducted. By providing an overview of the interview, clients are aware of the path that they will follow.

  As an example, this could be stated as follows:

  > "As part of the appointment, I will start off by asking you a series of questions to ensure that I understand the issue and the surrounding details. I will likely make notes during this part of the process to simply allow me to refer back to anything that you have mentioned. I will then be able to advise you regarding the legal position before I give you some guidance as to the options that are available to progress the matter further. I will then look at the next steps and advise on matters of ongoing funding. Is that okay?"

7.7.3 Initial Questioning and Listening

Perhaps one of the most significant challenges for the legal interviewer is ensuring that the client is given an opportunity to speak about the matter. Too often, the temptation is very much present to wish to pick up the initial thread of a client's problem and then instantly step in to seek to solve the matter. This could be a particular issue for any interviewer who has been provided with a 25-minute timeframe to complete the whole process by the SRA.

However, it is very important when it comes to the gathering of information to employ tactics that allow you to question openly, listen carefully, and then direct the conversation using closed questions to ensure that you have the information that you need to advise correctly.

There is also a very important role here for non-verbal communication, both in encouraging the client to speak and also to ensure that the client knows when you need to interject.

The whole stage begins with the first question, which needs to be an open question that encourages the client to detail the situation to you in their own words. There are many ways that this can be achieved. However, it is important to avoid a number of possible pitfalls.

For example:

- It is important to avoid an opening question that raises misplaced hope in a client – "Tell me about your case, and don't worry, we'll have this all sorted out for you".
- It is similarly important to avoid being overly negative either – "From looking at the details, this does seem rather a challenging situation, could you tell me more about how we got here?"
- It is also important to make sure that the client has confidence in you as a legal advisor, so anything which may undermine that should be avoided – "So . . . this . . . is the . . . er . . . oh, hang on . . . oh, it's the matter with the will, isn't it?" or "So, where shall we start, then?" Both of these would clearly be less than ideal.
- Of course, it is also possible that the start of the interview could be characterised by too much confidence – "I have looked through the papers, and it seems clear to me that . . ." – simply suggests an advisor who is not interested in listening.

At the same time, it is important, particularly in light of the SQE2 assessment, that you are aware of the need to be flexible to the matter at hand, and so the first question may need to be more general or more specific, dependent upon the information that you are provided with at the start of the 10-minute preparation period.

If, for example, you are given a very scant amount of detail, then a more general question would be advised:

> "I note that you are here regarding a family matter. Could you please tell me some more about how I can help?"

However, if the information provides more of a guide, then a more focused initial question would be appropriate:

> "I can see that you are here to discuss your will. Could you please start by telling me a little about what you would like your will to deal with?"

Once the client outlines the reason for their visit, the interviewer then needs to ensure that they strike the correct balance between a number of often opposing requirements – active listening, note-taking, directing the conversation, and thinking of the next question that may be needed.

The balance of this range of skills is often the most challenging at the start of a legal career. Often, the inexperienced interviewer will seek to prioritise one of the requirements over another, under the impression that a perfect set of interview notes is clearly the goal, only to find that they are getting less and less from a client who does not feel that they are being listened to. Equally, the highly attentive interviewer often ends the appointment and finds that their notes are incomplete and essential information has been missed.

It is therefore recommended to ensure, prior to the SQE2 assessment, that considerable time is devoted to practising these skills. By simply working with a friend or family member, you will be able to get clear advice on how your approach came across to an interviewee. It can also be helpful, although rather uncomfortable at times, to consider the use of technology as a means to record a practice interview with a view to allowing you to see yourself in action. This can be an important means of ensuring that you are able to identify issues and then practice further as a means to resolve them.

One further consideration that is often observable in inexperienced interviewers is the wish to be formulaic. This often takes the form of being comfortable asking an initial open question and then following this with often very direct closed questioning. This wish to follow a very clear and directed structure often impacts upon the interviewee negatively. Instead, it is always advisable to work to maintain as open an approach to questioning as you can for as long as you can prior to using closed questions to check details and gather missed information.

Whilst also helping the client to maintain their narrative, the use of open questions extended throughout the interview assists in providing the interviewer with time to think and reflect upon the information. It is also the case that clients are often at their most relaxed when they are talking – the notion of a problem shared is a problem halved.

The use of effective structure is important as your questions should naturally flow from the client's answers and should not be subject to sudden questions of a random or indiscriminate nature, which can wrong-foot the interviewee. It is advised instead to ensure that questions logically follow the information that you are provided with, as this will aid flow and client recall and will also assist your own internal process of filling in the information that you need to be able to consider the legal ramifications of the matter at hand.

Of course, at times, you do need to move between different topics. Where this is needed, it is advised to always clearly guide your client via short statements:

> "Many thanks for the information regarding the estate. Could you now tell me more about your mother's will?"

One final consideration in this opening questioning session is the need to remember that your client is an everyday human being. This may seem an obvious point to make, but it is often observed that interviewers can become fixated on the process and can forget that the person sitting before them will have thoughts, feelings, fears, anxieties, and needs and wants in regards to the situation presented to you. Do not be afraid to ask a client directly about these areas, as this will be of significant assistance as you continue the interview and in providing an ongoing legal service.

Example questions could include:

- "How does that make you feel?"
- "Do you foresee any specific problems in bringing a claim against Terry?"
- "Could you let me know of any particular concerns that you have about challenging the executors?"

7.7.4 Questioning for Detail

With an effective introduction provided, with rapport established, and with open questions helping to ensure that we have an active client who is sharing the details of the case with us, we then reach the next stage – making sure that we are now getting the right information to allow us to undertake our role.

Often, clients will spend significant time informing the legal advisor of significant amounts of information that they think are relevant but often turn out to not have any bearing at all on the legal aspects of the case at hand.

At this point, you have to always remember that the client came to be sitting across the desk from you as they did not know how to resolve the matter themselves. They are not legally trained, and they are not aware of the exact information that is vital to you being able to advise them appropriately.

It is, therefore, our role to guide them towards the information that we need, and this requires the interview to have a change of focus at the required time.

The change that is needed is to move from a passive and open style of dialogue with the client to a more active and directed approach that seeks to guide the narrative further. The concept of 'the required time' is more difficult to define, as this will always be a matter that has to be considered within the confines of the specific circumstances presented.

A useful approach to this section is to align the information provided in a manner that allows for the gaps to be seen and for the conversation to be more focused on the gaps that exist. This can take the form of the advisor taking a moment to summarise the information given so far. This allows the interviewer to reflect upon their notes, ensures that the client has the feeling that they have been heard, and, perhaps most importantly, gives a moment where you can think clearly and see what information has been missed.

It is then a simple task of asking the client to provide information that fills the gaps in a structured manner. The summary approach also allows the advisor to identify any inconsistencies in the story to date, and it may also assist in helping the client identify any area of the story where they may have missed a key fact that requires consideration.

Within the context of the assessment itself, the assessor will have a full back story that they will provide to you in response to the questions posed. This allows for an assessment of your questioning and listening skills in line with the assessment criteria. In particular, marks can be awarded under the following criteria:

- Listen to the client and use questioning effectively to enable the client to tell the solicitor what is important to them.
- Demonstrate client-focus in their approach to the client and the issues (i.e., demonstrate an understanding of the problem from the client's point of view and what the client wants to achieve, not just from a legal perspective).

7.7.5 The Advice Stage

It is important to always look to ensure that each of the stages of the interview process is completed using a staged approach. This is particularly important when we consider the advice stage of the meeting, as any advice given without being fully aware of the facts is likely to be an approach that could lead to professional negligence concerns further down the line.

With the questioning stage complete, the interview moves to an important phase where the dominant aspect of the appointment moves from the client imparting information to one where the legal advisor is required to take centre stage.

This can be a sizeable task – depending upon the client, the client's level of legal sophistication, and also the complexity of the matter at hand. It is therefore suggested that a structure within this area be employed to assist in building layers of information.

This is further supported by paragraph 8.6 of the SRA Code of Conduct, which states that,

> You give clients information in a way they can understand. You ensure they are in a position to make informed decisions about the services they need, how their matter will be handled and the options available to them.

The suggested approach is, therefore, to outline:

- The legal position
- Consideration of any relevant procedural steps
- Options for progressing the case

7.7.5.1 The Legal Position

The starting point to the advice section is often well aligned with a clear summary of the client's instructions that were discussed previously. Following an overview of the facts, the legal advisor is then well-positioned to complete three specific actions:

1. An accurate explanation of the client's legal rights and responsibilities – the general stage
2. The application of that law to the matter at hand – the specific stage
3. The deferral stage, in anticipation of further evidence or information

Taking each of these in turn.

- The general stage
  The SQE2 assessment requires that you are able to "Communicate and explain in a way that is suitable for the client to understand",[1] and this is where candidates may well be tested in their ability to communicate legal provisions to an everyday client.

With this in mind, it is advised to always be careful of using legal jargon that may not be understood by the client. Often, interviews in the area of Wills and Probate may lead to students straying into the discussion of legislation, such as the Wills Act 1837, the Administration of Estates Act 1925, or the Inheritance (Provision for Family and Dependants) Act 1975, all of which create potential barriers to trust or obstacles to clear communication and understanding.
However, this can also be the case when we use pseudo-legal terms such as capacity, validity, or intestacy. Where we look to use these terms, they should be clearly defined or should be avoided, and the definition should be used in their place. As an example:

> "For a will to have legal effect, it must be signed in a way that complies with the rules regarding who can sign, when they sign and how the process is completed".

Once we have informed the client about the law, we then need to make sure that we relate that law directly to the client's concerns.

- **The specific stage**
  The client has, of course, attended their appointment on the basis of discovering how the death of a loved one and the handling of their estate may be impacted by Inheritance Tax. They have not attended a lecture on the subject of death duties.
  It is, therefore, important to strike a balance between making sure that the client knows what the law says on a subject, but this must then be related directly to the facts of the case at hand.
  A useful approach here is to look to use the client's own words, or a paraphrased version of these, in the giving of specific advice.
  Following on from the previous example:

  > "I note that you mentioned that when you first saw the will, the signature appeared to have been amended".

- **The deferral stage**
  The SRA Assessment specification states that candidates:

  > [D]o not need to provide detailed advice at this stage. They can conduct the interview on the basis that they will be advising the client in detail at a later date. However, candidates do need to give enough preliminary advice and to address enough of the client's concerns to establish the client's trust and confidence.[2]

  It is, therefore, important to go into the assessment knowing that you are not expected to provide definitive advice unless it is clearly justified by the facts provided. This may, therefore, require consideration of what you may say to a client as a means of explaining why the advice is limited at this stage. An example would be:

> "Whilst it may be the case that we have a clear approach to move the matter forward, I am going to need to see the exact wording of the will before I can advise in detail".[3]

7.7.5.2 Procedural Considerations

The SQE2 assessments are based on either the area of property law and practice or on the area of wills and the administration of estates. Both of these areas have significant aspects of them that involve systematic procedural considerations. It is, therefore, important that your preparation includes revisiting areas such as the basic steps involved in the completion of a residential conveyance or perhaps the steps involved in the division of property under the rules of intestacy.

In interviews within the workplace, the outlining of procedural steps can be vital in helping to manage the client relationship, particularly where a process necessitates a number of stages over a period of time. If we have outlined these stages and the likely timeframes involved at the outset, then it can save considerable anxiety and questions at a later point.

7.7.5.3 Options for Progressing the Case

Whilst it can often be tempting to want to move a matter forward along the lines that we, as legal professionals, would consider appropriate, it is always helpful to recall that legal advisors are much like taxi drivers.

When you engage a taxi driver and then sit in the cab, you do not expect the cabbie to begin to drive you to the destination that they think you should go to. Instead, you give them an instruction, and it is their role to follow that and take you to that location.

Solicitors are largely the same.

So, whilst we may have a strong belief that there is a particular route that is best in the circumstances, it is for our clients to direct where they wish for us to go.

Once again, it is advisable to look at this area as one that can be best approached in a structured fashion.

- Step One – Outline feasible options
  It is important to ensure that the client is provided with a range of possible options that are relevant to the case. It is important to always state options that

involve both legal and non-legal approaches. It is often the case that options tend to boil down to a range of categories:

- "The full legal" – where the client is willing to engage legal services from the outset and has the means to opt for this route, or the route itself requires a full legal approach to proceed.
- "The pseudo legal" – where the matter is such that the use of external mediators, or alternative means of ADR, will likely suffice as a means to resolution.
- "The self-led" – used in situations where the case suggests that the parties involved could reach a resolution without the need to engage external support.
- "The do nothing" – a surprising response, but in a significant number of situations, there is actually no requirement to take a step towards action. Where this applies, it is always worth ensuring that a client is aware that they are under no obligation to take a specific step. It may also be the case that the client may be unable to choose one of the other options due, for example, to lack of funds.

- Step Two – Evaluate the advantages and disadvantages of each option
  With the possible choices outlined, it is then helpful to ensure that a brief consideration is given as to the relative merits of the options. It should be noted that these are often closely linked throughout. For example, whilst an advantage of doing nothing may be that it ensures that the client does not incur costs, suffer with stress, or be faced with a lengthy and possibly protracted legal battle. It is just as true to say that these are clear disadvantages of taking the full legal approach. On the contrary, whilst the full legal route may, for example, allow a client to assert their strict legal rights in regards to a deceased's estate. The option to do nothing ensures that this will not be the case.
- Step Three – Manage client expectations
  Linked with step two is the requirement to ensure that client expectations are managed in terms of the selection of a particular pathway. This requires that we are able to give helpful information about the implications of choosing a particular option in terms of timeframes, costs, commercial risks, anxiety, health considerations, personal and professional relationships, and even possible adverse publicity. A clear summary of what a client should expect helps to ensure that the client is committed to their course of action and understands how the matter will impact upon them.
- Step Four – Encourage the client to make a decision
  Within this step, it is important to note at the outset that there is a difficult balance to strike between encouraging and leading. What we are seeking here is an approach that ensures that we are aware of the client's initial thoughts on the options available. A suggested approach is to ask the client:

  > "In light of the options available, what are your initial thoughts on how you may like to proceed?"

This should hopefully allow for an open discussion of what the client's aims may be. This can be very helpful as we move towards the closing of the interview and any elements of action planning.

However, it is important to be wary of the client reversing the question:

> "What would you do?"

Of course, we have to go back to being a taxi driver at this point, and any response should be constrained to repeating the legal position, how this applies to the case, and whether the case has initial merit.

7.7.6 Concluding and Client Care

Regardless of whether the client has selected an option to pursue or has gone away to consider the detailed information and extensive range of options available in more detail, it will still be essential to ensure that the interview is concluded in an appropriate fashion. This requires ensuring that the client is aware of fees and disbursements, as well as action planning and client care considerations.

- Fees and disbursements

  As mentioned previously, it is often established practice to commence the interview by stating that the interview itself will be provided at no cost to the client. However, as we have gathered further information about the matter at hand, we are likely approaching the end of the appointment with enough information to provide the client with some guide as to the costs that may be involved.

  Paragraph 8.7 of the Code of Conduct states that:

  > You ensure that clients receive the best possible information about how their matter will be priced and, both at the time of engagement and when appropriate as their matter progresses, about the likely overall cost of the matter and any costs incurred.

  Noting the SQE2 assessment topics, it may well be the case that we need to ensure that we are aware of a range of different funding approaches. So, for example, if the enquiry related to a simple conveyance, then this may well be offered to a client on a fixed fee basis. In addition, this same approach is likely to apply if the matter relates to the drafting of a will. However, if we are required to advise upon a contentious will matter that may involve ongoing litigation, then this would likely require our initial interview to touch upon our hourly rate, and some guidance will be needed on the likely number of hours that may be involved.

  Of course, it may be the case that we need substantial initial information from the client to allow for an estimate of time to be provided. In these circumstances, it would be appropriate to simply provide the hourly rate and confirm that an estimate of charges will be provided as soon as possible – post the review of additional information.

At times, even with all the required information, it may still be difficult to ascertain with any accuracy the likely charges that the client would incur. So, if, for example, a solicitor was tasked with reaching a negotiated settlement on a matter, it may be required to confirm that:

> "It is difficult to provide an accurate estimate of how much time it will take to conclude the negotiation, and so it will not be possible to provide an outline cost at this point. We would, therefore, typically work on the basis that the total cost is likely to be in excess of £800, and I will ensure that you are kept informed about the costs involved as the matter progresses".

In addition to providing an overview of costs, it is also important that the client is aware of any and all disbursements that the case is likely to require. Again, it is important to define such a term with reference to the specific items that may apply, such as court fees or expert reports.

- Action planning
  It is helpful to ensure that a summary is provided to the client that ensures that both parties are aware of the steps that are to be taken immediately after the interview.
  By its very nature, this step is going to be case specific.
  However, consideration should be given to:
  - Any actions that have been agreed with the client at this stage.
  - Any time frames that have been agreed.
  - Any specific tasks that have been assigned to either the client or the solicitor.
- Client care
  The concluding parts of any legal interview should ensure that client care details are provided to the client. These should include:
  - Alternative contact details.
  - Confirmation of a client care letter and its content.
  - Specific confirmation about the firm's complaints procedure.

  This is also a good opportunity to ensure that all contact details have been gathered and confirmed and that we know the client's communication preferences. This can also be a useful time to ensure that we are aware of any particular needs that the client may have.

The appointment should then end with confirmation of the initial next step – usually when contact will next be made. In a real-life situation, you would then typically escort your client back to reception and bid them good day. In terms of the SQE2 assessment, it tends to be advised that you signal to your assessor that the interview is concluded, and simply standing up and thanking the 'client' for their time is an appropriate approach to this.

7.8 Effective Relationships – The Concept of Trust and Confidence

The final SRA performance indicator for the SQE2 assessment in interviewing states that candidates must:

> Establish and maintain an effective relationship with the client so as to build trust and confidence.

This is accompanied by a description of the type of behaviours that would demonstrate competence, which reads:

> The candidate effectively manages the client's expectations/circumstances, e.g. balances the client's objectives against what can be achieved within the timeframe; the client feels confident that the matter is in good hands and will be progressed.

Whilst some aspects of the assessment are perhaps simple to be able to identify within steps, approaches, or content that be prepared and practised prior to the day, it may be that trust and confidence are perhaps the most challenging of the skills required as it must pervade all aspects of the interview assessment.

From the very first moment where you greet the assessor as your client, you are required to create a professional rapport, and that starts with everything from your appearance to the first words that you use to place your client at ease within the interview setting. As you then proceed to introduce yourself and then move on to that initial question and the way that you work to gather the required information, at each stage, the trust and confidence that the client has within you is either being built or eroded.

Of course, this measure of trust and confidence will also be subtly adjusted in response to your non-verbal approach. Do you show that you are listening? Do you demonstrate empathy appropriately? Do you show understanding in your responses? Do you give the client the attention and level of professionalism expected?

Perhaps the most vital stage is the part of the interview where the candidate has the required information and can proceed to show their knowledge of the law, how that law applies to the client's matter, and also how options are provided and evaluated.

All of these elements combine to show the SQE assessor whether you are competent in demonstrating the skills of a day one solicitor in your approach to the interview. It is therefore advisable to spend considerable time seeking to practice the skills needed to establish and maintain trust, and this could be achieved via practice with friends, family, or peers, seeking a role within the legal sector where you can be exposed to clients, or through working within a legal advice centre.

Like driving a car on a road, we get better the more that we are exposed to real-life situations that we can reflect upon and learn from.

7.9 The Pervasive Nature of Ethics and Conduct

One of the other considerable challenges of the assessment is the potential for the SQE interviewing to require you to consider ethical and professional conduct issues within the scenario. To be clear, this is not a challenge because of the fact that it involves potential ethics and conduct issues, but because such issues will not arise in each assessment scenario, they have the ability to catch candidates unaware and can wrong foot a well-planned interview.

It is therefore important to ensure that preparation for the interview includes some consideration of the possible ethical and conduct issues which could arise in matters involving property or wills.

Examples include:

- A solicitor being asked to advise another party involved in the matter or the proposed transaction. This could be a request to act for both a buyer and a seller in a property purchase, acting for joint buyers, or being asked to act on behalf of both a borrower and a lender in the same matter.
- A request from a testator to make provisions within a will for a gift to be made to the solicitor themself.
- The possibility of money laundering concerns being raised in the provision of a deposit to the solicitor.
- The giving of will instructions by a person other than the testator.

It is, therefore, important to ensure that you have a working knowledge of both the duty to avoid conflicts of interest and the duty of confidentiality. It would also be advisable to ensure that you have looked over details from *The Money Laundering, Terrorist Financing and Transfer of Funds (Information on the Payer) Regulations 2017*.

7.10 Negotiation

Another potential outlier in the SQE2 interview assessment process is the topic of negotiation.

As stated in the SRA's SQE2 Assessment Specification:

> Although there is no separate assessment called negotiation, all deliveries of SQE2 will contain at least one assessment involving negotiation. Negotiation may be assessed in either interview and attendance note/legal analysis and/or case and matter analysis and/or legal writing.

It is, therefore, important that we are aware of the requirement to potentially identify and advise parties upon negotiated settlement options.

7.11 Note-Taking in Assessment

The completion of the whole assessment for SQE2 requires the candidate to demonstrate both the skills of legal interviewing and of attendance note writing and legal analysis.

It is, therefore, vital that you are accustomed to preparing contemporaneous notes during an interview, as it would be incredibly difficult to complete the second aspect of the assessment without some notes to work from.

It should be noted that the performance indicators for the Attendance Note/Legal Analysis component state that a candidate must demonstrate the skill of recording all relevant information.

Candidates would be advised to practice the taking of notes within interview settings, either through formal interview experience or through practising with peers, family, or friends. The aim is to create a clear, legible, and structured set of notes that align with the requirements of the attendance note format.

As noted previously, it can be challenging to build rapport, actively listen, guide the interview structure, think of questions, and write notes simultaneously. However, these are the skills that are required within the role of the legal professional.

7.12 Time Factors

The starting point to considering time is to note again that the assessment interview is limited to 25 minutes in duration. This may seem a short amount of time to complete a legal interview, but there are two points to consider. Firstly, you are given information in advance of the appointment and 10 minutes of preparation time; these are vital to use effectively if you are going to have a successful outcome within the assessment and have been covered earlier in this chapter. The second consideration is that the SRA is not trying to catch you out with the time frame allocated. The question writers will have prepared a brief which allows students to complete all of the required stages within the time available.

With this in mind, within this chapter, we have sought to provide a structured approach that is designed to allow candidates to demonstrate the range of skills and knowledge required.

However, the structure does require your awareness of time as you proceed – as you can imagine, it is difficult to predict an exact response that you will receive to one of your questions, and it is likely that all legal professionals have, at times, sat back and listened for an extended period of time to a response from a client that was significantly more than the question itself warranted.

It is, therefore, important to ensure that you keep a close track on timings as you proceed. A handy way of doing this is to make a note of the interview start time at the start of the session. By writing this down at the very top of the page, you have a quick visual point to refer to as a means of tracking where the appointment has reached.

With time a consideration, you should be able to then work to create an effective balance of time allocated within each segment of the assessment. However, with the best will in the world, not everything can ever go to plan, no matter how specific the plan may be.

With that in mind, candidates need to be able to move to plan B, should the circumstances require.

So, for example, if time is running out, it may be better to seek to conclude the interview in the appropriate fashion rather than to be cut off in mid-sentence by the assessor as time has elapsed.

Whilst it never feels ideal to cut a segment short, it can help to leave a more positive thought in the mind of the assessor than seeming to suggest that you had no knowledge of time at all.

As a suggestion, the following approach may assist:

> "Thank you for your initial thoughts on the options discussed. If you decide to proceed with the case, then we can arrange a further meeting to look at the options in more detail. Now, before we finish, can I just ask if you have any further areas that need clarification?"

The areas that perhaps were not able to be considered in full detail can then be recorded on the attendance note.

Exercises

There now follows two example interviews. The first is based upon a property matter, followed by a wills and probate scenario.

In getting the most out of the exercises, we advise using the approach detailed previously, which is repeated here in summary.

Plan a structure for the interview:

> During the 10-minute preparation time, you should draw a plan on how you are going to structure the interview. If you are given any documents, please read those very carefully and include any relevant information or advice in your plan.

As the assessment criteria for interviewing are primarily based on skills, you should plan a structure based on those criteria. For example, you should plan how you are going to demonstrate the following skills:

- Listening and questioning
- Communicating and explaining
- Conducting professionally and treating the client with respect and politeness
- Demonstrating client-focus
- Building trust and confidence

You must be prepared to adapt as the interview progresses. This is because a piece of new information may emerge, or the client's approach or expectation may change.

A good interview can follow different styles. However, you should note a few key points. For example, you should begin with an **introduction**. This should be followed by **a short description of your knowledge about the case, asking questions and listening to the answers and responses, advising and answering any questions, and concluding the interview**. You should structure the interview to demonstrate the skills set in the assessment criteria. You can do this by planning a structured interview where the key points are embedded.

- **Introduction:** Your interview should begin with a very good introduction. A good idea is to start building rapport with the client by asking how they travelled to the firm or if they had any trouble finding the firm. This can put the client at ease. You should then introduce yourself by telling them who you are and your relationship with the firm. You should also inform the client that your firm is regulated by the SRA. You should then share the agenda of the meeting. For example, you can state that today's meeting is to find out some information from the client and understand the client's case. So, you will be asking some questions. Please also make them aware that you will be taking notes. If you have any note-takers or colleagues attending, you should introduce them too to the client and explain their role. Explain that any information shared in the meeting by the client will be kept confidential. You should also inform them that you may have to ask them to slow down or pause while taking notes so the relevant information can be noted down. Please reassure the client that if they need any clarification or if they want you to repeat any question, they can do that. Ensure that you inform them that they can ask questions at any time during the interview, but you suggest that they ask questions at the end because they can be answered better after knowing the relevant information. You should then give them the necessary legal advice and inform them of 'what would happen next'.

- **A short description:** You should confirm the nature of the dispute or case. This can be done by confirming the 'reason for the visit' to the client, which you may have a memo, an e-mail, or a fax. For instance, in the property law example, you can say, "I understand that you have received a mortgage default notice from your lender, and you wanted to discuss this with us". You can also check and confirm personal details such as title, name, date of birth (if necessary), occupation, address, and national insurance number.
- **Listening and questioning:** It is very important to listen to your client carefully so you can ask the appropriate questions to discover the important information that you would need to advise the client. Showing that you are an attentive listener also encourages the client to tell what is important to them. So, use appropriate body language by maintaining good eye contact, nodding, and using confirmatory phrases like "so it was a repayment mortgage" or "so your brother owned the house in his sole name". Always listen to your client in a non-judgemental manner, providing reassurance when appropriate and allowing them to raise concerns. Listening carefully will also help you with note-taking and getting a good knowledge of the relevant legal and factual issues.

  Ask appropriate questions that would bring the relevant information out from the client. Please note that the client will not automatically give all the necessary information, and some information may be withheld by them if you do not ask the appropriate question. More importantly, use the words and phrases that the client can clearly understand. If the client does not seem to understand your question, repeat it and be prepared to explain what you want to know. Questions can be closed, open, or a mixture of both. Please remember that you need to take the lead of the interview as you only have 25 minutes to conduct the interview, and some information may not be relevant or important. Good questioning techniques will identify any gaps and ambiguities that are present in the client's case and elicit the information required to advise the client. It will also gain a clear understanding of the client's account of the case. Please do not forget to ask the client what they want to achieve. This will not only demonstrate your client-focused approach but also enable you to give advice focusing on the client's needs.
- **Advising and answering:** Effective communication is the key skill that you need to demonstrate by advising the client and answering any questions from them. You should begin by setting out the strengths and weaknesses of the case before advising on further action and pointing out the consequences of such action. Please ensure that you give the correct advice because you must not mislead the client as to the facts or law. Please also ensure that you have dealt with all of the issues raised explicitly or implicitly in your brief.

  Answer the client's question effectively. You can do this by making queries such as whether they understand your answer, whether they have any more questions on this, or whether they have understood everything that has been discussed in the meeting. If the client asks for your opinion, which you cannot give without further legal research or expert opinion, you can say that to them. However, do not hold back anything which you are sure about. For instance, certainly, a bank can legally serve a notice of default to the borrowers when they fail to keep up their mortgage repayments. Do not forget to check that you have the necessary information that you need from the client. Finally, obtain your client's instructions as to how they wish to proceed.

- **Conclusion:** Once you are sure that you have all the information that you need from the client, you should inform them what will happen next. You can tell them that you will undertake some legal research and discuss the case with your supervisor, a senior partner, or an expert counsel. You will then decide whether to take the case on and, if so, how legal costs should be covered. Please note that you do not need to discuss legal costs with the client at the interview; you will outline legal costs in the client care letter. Once you have done these, you must inform the client that the meeting ends there.

  In addition to the previous, you must demonstrate that you conduct the interview in a professional manner and treat the client with courtesy, respect, and politeness, including respecting diversity where relevant. Where there is an inadequate demonstration of professionalism and courtesy or respect towards the client, you may find yourself in breach of the SRA code of conduct, which may lead to failing the assessment. For instance, do not unnecessarily interrupt the client and/or use inappropriate body language, i.e., responding aggressively or showing a lack of interest in their response. Please always bear in mind that the key objective of the interview is to build the client's trust and confidence.

Conduct a Practice Interview!

In both of the scenarios that follow, you have received some initial instructions from your firm's secretary on how to conduct the interview (see facsimile e-mail messages from your firm's secretary). This allows you to conduct a practice interview with a friend or family member who can act as the client and assessor. While you must read the assessment criteria and how the assessor will apply those to grade the interview, you **MUST NOT** read the client's instructions before interviewing because they contain the information that you will have to elicit from the client. You can share and discuss the assessment criteria (outlined later) and client instructions (see further on) with your friend or family member. They must read these documents before starting the meeting. While they read the documents, please prepare an interview plan within the 10-minute preparation time. It is a good idea to record the meeting so you can listen to it later and find where you could improve. Please ensure that your interview is concluded within 25 minutes. Please note that finishing your interview too early may have a negative impact on your grade.

Assessment Criteria and Grading

An assessor, who will play the role of the client, will assess the candidate. The assessment criteria for interviewing skills refer to skills, NOT application of the law (see further on). Candidates' performance in the interview will be assessed against the following criteria:

1. Listen to the client and use questioning effectively to enable the client to tell the solicitor what is important to them.
2. Communicate and explain in a way that is suitable for the client to understand.
3. Conduct themselves in a professional manner and treat the client with courtesy, respect, and politeness, including respecting diversity where relevant.
4. Demonstrate client-focus in their approach to the client and the issues (i.e., demonstrate an understanding of the problem from the client's point of view and what the client wants to achieve, not just from a legal perspective).
5. Establish and maintain an effective relationship with the client so as to build trust and confidence.

Performance in each of the preceding criteria will be assessed on a scale from A – F by trained assessors making global professional judgments related to the standard of competency of the assessment as follows:

A. Superior performance: well above the competency requirements of the assessment
B. Clearly satisfactory: clearly meets the competency requirements of the assessment
C. Marginal pass: on balance, just meets the competency requirements of the assessment
D. Marginal fail: on balance, just fails to meet the competency requirements of the assessment
E. Clearly unsatisfactory: clearly does not meet the competency requirements of the assessment
F. Poor performance: well below the competency requirements of the assessment.

This grading will then be converted into numerical marks such that A = 5 marks and F = 0 marks.

EXERCISE A

Example Property Interview

Property Interview

CLIENT INTERVIEWING SKILLS
Moneyhive v McGregor

Subject Areas

Client interviewing skills
Property law (mortgage)

As a SQE 2 candidate and/or a trainee solicitor, you are expected to interview clients to elicit information, discuss their case, and offer some advice (if necessary).

Trainee solicitors are often asked to conduct client interviews on short notice, and you will often know very little about the case. So, you shall be prepared for this. You will, therefore, have to elicit the necessary information from the client, professionally conduct the interview, and build the client's trust and confidence.

You have to demonstrate that you have reached the standard of competency of a day one solicitor. This means that you can apply fundamental legal principles in the interview by addressing the client's needs and concerns. You are expected to know or address the details if they have been provided to you as part of the assessment. Additionally, you are expected to do the same that a day one solicitor would look up.

In this task, you will learn how to conduct an excellent client interview in a property law matter, i.e., mortgage. You will also learn what you need to be aware of while discussing the case with the client and giving advice.

Preparation

The power of sale by a mortgagee (lender): Law of Property Act 1925 ss. 101, 103.

The law on mortgages and the factors that the courts consider when deciding upon an application for a 'possession order' by the mortgagee and 'time order' by a mortgagor (borrower): Administration of Justice Act 1970, s. 36; Consumer Credit Act 1974, part IX.

Personal liability to outstanding mortgage debt which was not satisfied from the proceeds of sale: Limitation Act 1980 s 20.

You may find the Financial Services and Markets Act 2000 (FSMA) helpful in understanding the key features of regulated mortgage contracts.

Instructions

You received a message at 8.15am this morning (see what follows).

You have been informed that you should interview the client in the conferencing room located in your firm.

You should imagine that you will meet your client for the first time at 10.00am today.

You have 10 minutes to consider the e-mail and/or documents. Please see the section 'use of 10 minutes' (Chapter 7).

In the interview, you should aim to win the client's trust and confidence.

You should also try to obtain all the relevant information and as full an understanding as possible of the client's concerns. You do not need to provide detailed advice at this stage. You can conduct the interview on the basis that you will be advising the client in detail at a later date. However, you must provide some preliminary and essential advice at the meeting.

Assessment Objective

Candidates can demonstrate they are able to conduct an interview with a client.

WHEN CONSIDERING THE DOCUMENT THAT FOLLOWS, YOU HAVE 10 MINUTES TO PREPARE YOUR INTERVIEW

FACSIMILE E-MAIL MESSAGE

************ URGENT ************

From: Secretary, Borderland and Co Solicitors, London.
To: Trainee solicitor

I have made an appointment for you to meet with Mr Alexander McGregor.

The client has not used the firm before.

The client was very brief over the phone but did ask if you could provide him with some advice on a 'mortgage repayment default notice' that he received from their lender, Moneyhive Bank Ltd.

The client sounded particularly distressed over the phone, but I have assured them that you would be able to assist them with their query.

Remember, the firm charges your time at £150.00 plus VAT per hour. However, you should make the client aware that this first interview with yourself is free of charge. Any future work carried out by the firm will be charged at £300 plus VAT per hour.

You are to direct any further queries regarding the matter to your supervisor.

Please advise the client appropriately.

You will have up to 25 minutes to conduct the interview.

THE FOLLOWING DOCUMENT SHOULD NOT BE READ BY THE INTERVIEWER PRIOR TO THE INTERVIEW

Client Instructions (Mr McGregor)

Make sure that you learn the details of the client's situation and wishes before the interview. Do not give all of the information out at once: respond to any of the questions you are asked by making the solicitor/candidate prompt you for details.

If necessary, you may have to improvise to fill gaps in these instructions. Do not, however, invent facts that are inconsistent with these instructions.

Your Personal Details

Your name is Alexander McGregor. You are 45 years old (DOB: 30/04/1979). You were employed as a senior manager in a cinema for nearly a decade. Previously, you worked in a managerial role with different employers.

You are married to Ann-Marie McGregor. She is 42 years old (DOB: 10/01/1982). You have been married to her for 14 years. You have two children (Alan and Beccy) in the marriage; Alan is 12, and Beccy is 9 years old.

Your home address is 16 Topcliffe Road, Weyford, Guildshire, GU7 7FG. Telephone number 01930 71111. This is also the address of the mortgaged property.

You have already been informed that you will not be eligible for Community Legal Services funding. You have already told the trainee solicitor's secretary that you have no legal expenses insurance.

Reason for Visit

You recently received a default notice from your mortgage lender, Moneyhive Bank Ltd, which asked you to resume mortgage repayments by 1 May, or they will issue possession proceedings in the court. As you have been made redundant by your previous employer, you cannot make any repayments at the moment.

The Background (To Be Freely Volunteered)

You and your wife (Mrs McGregor) were saving money to buy a four-bedroom house in Guildshire. Due to the ever-increasing market value of houses in the area, you were struggling to save a 10% deposit. You and your wife registered with a mortgage broker who informed you that the government was backing a 95% mortgage, so they shall be able to buy their dream house if they can pay a

5% deposit of the purchase price. You both were very delighted to know this, as you and your wife's savings can pay a 5% deposit. You both instructed the mortgage broker to find a suitable mortgage lender. The broker found a lender called 'Moneyhive Bank Ltd' who agreed to lend you and your wife £380,000 to cover 95% of the purchase price under a mortgage.

In May 2023, you and your wife started house hunting but could not find your dream home within the catchment area of a primary and secondary school. This is because your children, Alan and Beccy, would need to attend a secondary and primary school, respectively. You and your wife also did not want to commute a long distance to your workplaces. In July 2023, you both contacted a local estate agent and instructed them to find a house that would meet your requirements. The estate agent found a semi-detached house in Guildshire, which was marketed at £400,000. You and your wife liked the house and the location. The house was purchased in August 2023 with a deposit of £20,000 (5% of the purchase price), and the remaining £380,000 was paid by taking a mortgage from Moneyhive.

To Be Disclosed If Asked

Half of the deposit (£10,000) was contributed by your wife, Mrs McGregor. The house is registered in the Land Registry in the joint names of you and your wife. The mortgage is registered in the Land Registry as a charge over the house. Since the purchase of the house, you have been paying the monthly mortgage repayment from your salary until you were made redundant in December last year. Your wife has been paying the utility bills, council tax, weekly shopping, car insurance, and childcare costs. You are actively looking for a job but without any success. Your wife is working, but her income is not enough to pay the full monthly mortgage repayment of £2,400. As a result, no repayments have been made since January 2024. You have received a few letters from Moneyhive asking to resume payments, but you could not. The most recent letter from Moneyhive asked you to resume payments by 1 May 2024, and failure to do so would result in an application for eviction in the county court.

The outstanding mortgage debt is £410,000. The market value of the house is currently £390,000. However, you feel that due to the current financial crisis, the house would not be sold at that price.

You have been in touch with your ex-girlfriend Marcela, who is a Michelin-starred chef in a five-star hotel in Canada. You also recently met her in London when she was visiting a friend, and she told you that she still loves you. When you told her about your situation, she offered you to move to her house in Canada. She also assured you that you can work with her in the kitchen as she always needs an assistant. You think this is a good offer and you would not need to worry about accommodation.

You have recently found out that your wife's grandfather left his house in a will to her, so she can easily pay off the mortgage debt with that inheritance and she and the children will have a roof over their heads.

You have also been offered a job as an assistant manager in a supermarket in Surrey, but the salary offered is much lower than your previous salary. It would not pay the monthly mortgage instalment after deductions i.e., pension contribution, tax, and NI.

What You Want

You want to know the following:

1. Can Moneyhive sell the house to recover the debt?
2. Is there any way to postpone the sale? If yes, for how long?
3. What is the likely outcome of the eviction notice?
4. If you leave the UK to move in with Marcela, would you still be liable for any outstanding mortgage debt?
5. You want assurance from the solicitor that they are not going to inform your secret plan of leaving the country to live with your ex-girlfriend.
6. You feel that 25 minutes is not enough time to discuss everything, so you offer the solicitor a few drinks after the meeting to chat about how you reconnected with your ex-girlfriend after all these years and why you think that she is the right person in your life. You told them that you will seriously consider instructing the firm if his offer is accepted.

EXERCISE B

Example Interview for Wills and Intestacy, Probate Administration and Practice

Wills and Intestacy, Probate Administration and Practice Interview

CLIENT INTERVIEWING SKILLS
Chris Turner

Subject Areas

Client interviewing skills
Wills and administration of estates (Intention, Formality and Inheritance (Provision for Family and Dependants) Act 1975.

As a SQE 2 candidate and/or a trainee solicitor, you are expected to interview clients to elicit information, discuss their case, and offer some advice (if necessary).

Trainee solicitors are often asked to conduct client interviews on short notice, and you will often know very little about the case. So, you should be prepared for this. You will, therefore, have to elicit the necessary information from the client, professionally conduct the interview, and build the client's trust and confidence.

You have to demonstrate that you have reached the standard of competency of a day one solicitor. This means that you can apply fundamental legal principles in the interview by addressing the client's needs and concerns. You are expected to know or address the details if they have been provided to you as part of the assessment. Additionally, you are expected to do the same that a day one solicitor would look up.

In this task, you will learn how to conduct a client interview in a wills matter. You will also learn what you need to be aware of while discussing the case with the client and giving advice.

Preparation

1. The requirements of a valid will. In order to make a valid will, a Testator must have the capacity to make a will, and the requirements of s.9 Wills Act 1837 must be complied with. There may be an issue under S9 in that both witnesses were not present at the same time.
2. How a client's intention is demonstrated in the drawing up of a will. This includes consideration of capacity and duress.
3. The requirements for making a valid claim under the Inheritance Act (Provision for Family and Dependants) Act.

Instructions

You received a message at 8.15am this morning (see what follows).

You have been informed that you should interview the client in the conferencing room located in your firm.

You should imagine that you will meet your client for the first time at 10.00 am today.

You have 10 minutes to consider the e-mail and/or documents. Please see the section 'use of 10 minutes' (Chapter 7).

In the interview, you should aim to win the client's trust and confidence.

You should also try to obtain all the relevant information and as full an understanding as possible of the client's concerns. You do not need to provide detailed advice at this stage. You can conduct the interview on the basis that you will be advising the client in detail at a later date. However, you must provide some preliminary and essential advice at the meeting.

Assessment Objective

Candidates can demonstrate they are able to conduct an interview with a client.

WHEN CONSIDERING THE DOCUMENT THAT FOLLOWS, YOU HAVE 10 MINUTES TO PREPARE YOUR INTERVIEW

FACSIMILE E-MAIL MESSAGE

************ URGENT ************

From: Secretary – Brown, Skinner and Ferret LLP, Southport.
To: Trainee solicitor
I have made an appointment for you to meet with Chris Turner.

The client has not used the firm before.

The client was very brief over the phone but did ask if you could provide him with some advice on the legal processes following the death of Chris's sister, Paige. Chris seemed unwilling to provide much further information but did mention that the deceased seems to have had two wills at the time of death that named two different beneficiaries.

The client sounded particularly distressed over the phone, but I have assured them that you would be able to assist them with their query.

Remember, the firm charges your time at £150.00 plus VAT per hour. However, you should make the client aware that this first interview with yourself is free of charge.

You are to direct any further queries regarding the matter to your supervisor.

Please advise the client appropriately.

You will have up to 25 minutes to conduct the interview.

THE FOLLOWING DOCUMENT *SHOULD NOT* BE READ BY THE INTERVIEWER PRIOR TO THE INTERVIEW

Instructions for the Client (Chris Turner)

Make sure that you learn the details of the client's situation and wishes before the interview. Do not give all of the information out at once: respond to any of the questions you are asked by making the solicitor/candidate prompt you for details.

If necessary, you may have to improvise to fill gaps in these instructions. Do not, however, invent facts that are inconsistent with these instructions.

Your Personal Details

Your name is Chris Turner. You are 65 years old (DOB: 30/04/19XX). Prior to your retirement, on medical grounds, you were employed as a porter at your local hospital.

You have never married and have no children.

Your home address is 15 Clarendon Street, Tarleton, Lancashire, PR1 1OG. Telephone number 01942 701701.

You have already been informed that you will not be eligible for Community Legal Services funding. You have already told the trainee solicitor's secretary that you have no legal expenses insurance.

Reason for Visit

Paige Turner, your older sister, passed away a week before this interview. It was your understanding that you were the sole beneficiary of Paige's will, and you, therefore, expected that the whole of her estate would pass to you if she were to pass away. The reason for your expectation is based upon a will that Paige executed 15 years ago following the death of her husband. After her husband's death, Paige was particularly keen to ensure that she had her own affairs in order, and she took the opportunity to involve you in the whole process. This included discussing her wishes, informing you that the will had been completed, and even giving you a copy of the will (you still have this at home).

This will left everything to you as her only living relative. Since Paige's death, you have been informed that she had executed a new will just a month before she died that states that she intends to leave the whole of her estate to a young man some 40 years younger than her. The young man in question is Eduardo, who Paige met on a recent holiday to Tunisia. You are very concerned about the revelation of the new will, and you seek advice on whether any steps can be taken to do something about it.

The Background (To Be Freely Volunteered)

You are Chris Turner of 15 Clarendon Street, Tarleton, Lancashire, PR1 1OG. You are the youngest child of Catherine and Jonathan Turner, and you had an older sister, Paige Turner, who died seven days before this interview.

Catherine passed away in 1996, Jonathan died in 2010, and you and Paige had no other relatives.

Around a year ago, Paige had started to become unwell. This happened around the time of her 73rd birthday and was characterised by a lack of mobility – Paige had real issues standing for any period of time – and issues with confusion, forgetfulness, and extended moments where Paige would seem to simply drift away into her own world.

Paige was aware of her health issues, and during her more lucid moments, she looked to see if there were any treatment options that may assist. However, she was not comfortable with taking medication and had a deep mistrust of doctors. Due to this, she was open to looking at alternative treatment methods that were based on nature, meditation, and cleansing. Through a local healer, she had been informed about a retreat in Tunisia that specialised in a range of therapies that she hoped would assist. It was at the retreat that she met Eduardo, and when she returned to the UK, he came back with her under the guise of providing ongoing therapy.

In the weeks that followed, Chris visited Paige on a number of occasions, and it was clear that the alternative therapy was having no positive effect. In fact, it appeared to Chris that she was actually declining at an even more rapid rate. With some pressure, Chris managed to get Paige to visit her GP, much against the wishes of Eduardo.

However, after the first GP appointment, Chris was unable to then get Paige to revisit the GP and access treatment. This was largely stopped by Eduardo, who would come up with a range of excuses to stop Chris from spending time with Paige. When Chris would visit, Eduardo would tell Chris that Paige was asleep, resting, or in meditation and could not be disturbed.

The same situation occurred when Chris attempted to telephone Paige. Every time, the call would be answered by Eduardo, and a similar range of excuses would be given.

Chris did not give up and, on rare occasions, did manage to get to see Paige. On these occasions, it was apparent that she was becoming more and more confused, and this left Chris feeling even more concerned. Over the years, Chris had become a familiar face to the neighbours, and during one visit, he was stopped in the street by Tony Mamil, who lived next door.

Tony told Chris that Eduardo had knocked on his door to ask if Tony would sign a document for Paige. Tony had always liked Paige, and so he was happy to help and followed Eduardo back to Paige's house. Tony said hello, and Paige replied by asking Eduardo, "Who is this?" This surprised Tony as he and Paige had been good neighbours for over 10 years. Eduardo then put the document in front of Paige and got her to sign. He then asked Tony to sign as well, which he did.

Although Tony does not know what the document was, he did see that it had already been signed by someone else before either Paige or Tony had signed it. Tony also mentioned that Eduardo shouted at Paige as she hesitated to sign, and she seemed to be frightened of the younger man.

Since the death of Paige, Eduardo has provided a copy of the new will to Chris. The new will is signed by Paige, Tony, and Mrs Ruth Slate. The will leaves the whole of the estate to Eduardo and names Eduardo and his brother Stan as the executors.

To Be Disclosed If Asked

If asked the date of death, give a date exactly one week ago.

Paige's estate comprised:

- Her home at 21 Withington Street, Birkdale, Southport, PR9 1PB, is worth approximately £415,000. The house is owned outright, and there is no ongoing mortgage
- Bank/Building Society Accounts with total balances is £171,000
- Shares in McDonald Homes worth approximately £137,000

Mrs Ruth Slate lives at number 25 Withington Street, in Birkdale, Southport. Ruth has been spoken to and confirms that she was asked to sign a document by Eduardo. This was signed in the street, and Paige was not present at the time.

Eduardo has instructed a firm of solicitors to deal with the process of probate. They are Cheat, Steal, and Prosper LLP of Bispham Road, Churchtown, Southport, PR9 1DL. They hold the original copy of the new will.

You do not have contact details for Eduardo.

Four years ago, you were medically retired from work due to a back complaint. Since that point, you have sought to access benefits, but your claim was rejected, and you have only been able to access basic benefits at this time. When Paige discovered this, she made provisions to support you financially. This included a payment direct to your landlord to cover your rent and a direct debit payment into your account to cover your bills and day-to-day expenses. This totals £400 per month. With Paige's death, you are now not receiving those payments, and you are worried about how you will afford to house and feed yourself without the payments from Paige.

The Client's Concerns

- Which of the wills is the correct will?
- If the new will is correct, is there anything that can be done to prevent Eduardo from inheriting the entire estate?

Self-Reflection Checklist

What three important things have you learnt from this chapter?	**1**	**2**	**3**
Set out the three additional steps that you need to take to learn the skills in this chapter in more detail.	**1**	**2**	**3**

Notes

1 Solicitors Regulation Authority, 'SQE2 Assessment Specification' (*sra.org.uk*, April 2024) <https://sqe.sra.org.uk/exam-arrangements/assessment-information/sqe2-assessment-specification> accessed 21 November 2024.

2 Solicitors Regulation Authority, 'SQE2 Assessment Specification' (*sra.org.uk*, April 2024) <https://sqe.sra.org.uk/exam-arrangements/assessment-information/sqe2-assessment-specification> accessed 21 November 2024.

3 Solicitors Regulation Authority, 'SQE2 Assessment Specification' (*sra.org.uk*, April 2024) <https://sqe.sra.org.uk/exam-arrangements/assessment-information/sqe2-assessment-specification> accessed 21 November 2024.

8 Legal Analysis and Attendance Notes

Key Chapter Points

1. This final chapter guides the reader to consider the importance of correct attendance note practice.
2. Attendance notes play a number of key roles within the legal process, and within the chapter, consideration is given to areas such as costing, professional negligence, working within a team, and case management.
3. Professional rules and codes of conduct are a constant within the role of the legal professional in the completion of attendance notes.
4. A competent legal professional carries out their role to the expected standards as set out by professional bodies and associated codes.
5. An ethical legal professional is expected to be honest, have integrity, and adhere to regulations and standards to maintain public trust and confidence in the profession.
6. There are many facets to the process of attendance note compilation, with no one correct approach.
7. The SQE requirements in this area require candidates to combine knowledge, skills, organisation, and time management to achieve a successful outcome.

8.1 Introduction

After conducting the SQE interview, candidates must then write up an attendance note which is required to contain a thorough legal analysis. Whilst it would be easy to think of the interview as perhaps the most challenging component within the SQE2 assessment, it should be noted that the completion of an interview, followed by a 25-minute written assessment of your note-taking, analysis, and attendance note process, has proved challenging for many.

Of course, attendance notes have been part of the process of the legal professional for as long as we have called upon others for legal advice. In practice, though, the attendance note is usually just a summary of the stage of the case and interactions and the time engaged by the solicitor. However, it is important to note that the

DOI: 10.4324/9781003519096-8

SQE assessment does require something more, as the assessment requires that the note includes an in-depth analysis and application of the legal concepts to the scenario.

It is also important to note that the use of digital record systems, as you would likely use in practice, are not replicated for SQE2. Instead, the attendance note that you are required to produce will be handwritten.

Within this chapter, we will consider the requirement of both practice and assessment to give the reader a detailed guide to attendance notes and legal analysis.

8.2 The SQE2 Attendance Note/ Legal Analysis Assessment

In considering the attendance note/legal analysis aspect of the assessment, it is important to note that the assessment criteria applied here are those from the written assessment specification.

The SRA Performance Indicators break the process down into five clear requirements, and these are aligned with statements of competence that are as follows:

Table 8.1 The SRA Performance Indicators

Skills	Indicators demonstrating competence
Record all relevant information	The candidate identifies and sets out the relevant facts contained in the assessment documents and elicited from the Client Interview, e.g., facts which are important in ensuring the client's needs/ objectives are met or relevant to the legal analysis
Identify appropriate next steps	The candidate sets out the steps to be taken to progress the client's matter, e.g., the solicitor will provide a letter of advice to the client or request further information from the client
Provide client-focused advice (i.e., advice which demonstrates an understanding of the problem from the client's point of view and what the client wants to achieve, not just from a legal perspective)	The candidate demonstrates an understanding of the client's concerns from the client's perspective (e.g., the candidate addresses the client's legal problems, any relevant commercial considerations, and/or the client's personal circumstances).
Apply the law correctly to the client's situation	Apply the law comprehensively to the client's situation, identifying any ethical and professional conduct issues and exercising judgment to resolve them honestly and with integrity

The SRA Assessment Specification provides more detailed guidance on the content of the document. This states that the following must be recorded:

- All relevant information obtained during the interview should be recorded in the attendance note/legal analysis record.
- Candidates should provide an analysis of any legal issues that arise in the matter and record their initial advice for the client.
- The attendance note/legal analysis should also identify the next steps to be taken by the solicitor and, where applicable, the client, as well as any ethical issues that arise and how they should be dealt with.
- This may (but will not necessarily) include options and strategies for negotiation.
- If the e-mail from the partner or secretary has asked the candidate to deal with any specific issues or questions, then advice on these issues should also be included.

As noted previously, this is an assessment that provides just 25 minutes and must be handwritten, and it is therefore important that submissions are clear, legible, and comprehensible – not a simple task when you have the requirements stated previously to consider.

In terms of language expectations, the SRA confirms the following:

- Answers should be clear, succinct, and use accurate language that avoids unnecessary technical terms where they are not appropriate.
- There is no spell check or highlighting function for the SQE2 written assessments.
- Candidates should not lose marks for spelling mistakes that:
    - Do not impact on the legal accuracy, clarity, and/or certainty of the written text; and would normally be flagged by spell check functionality, noting that spell check would not, for example, necessarily flag errors in names, addresses, dates, or values.
- Candidates should not lose marks for grammatical errors that:
    - Do not impact on the legal accuracy, clarity, and/or certainty of the written text, noting that, for example, grammatical errors in the use of tense could have such an impact; and
    - Do not make the written text inaccessible to the intended reader.
- Candidates should not lose marks for poor formatting, given the lack of formatting support on the test platform and the time restraints under which candidates are working.

In light of the SRA guidance on the assessment, it is important to consider a number of practical points to aid your preparation.

1. The attendance note provides a primary record of what was said during the interview. It is, therefore, vital to ensure that you maintain a sufficient set of notes during the interview to enable the completion of the formal record.
2. Even with the assessment being handwritten within a 25-minute timeframe, it is still a piece of professional writing, so it should be written to the appropriate standard. In practice, attendance notes are often read by your supervisor, senior colleagues, or even by defendant representatives (particularly in costs disputes). It is advisable to treat the assessment as though your note would be read by such an audience.
3. 25 minutes is a short timeframe to complete the process and, therefore, being concise in your completion of the task will be key to ensuring that you are able to meet the assessment requirements. The use of a bullet point approach is acceptable and can be a great help in saving time by avoiding narrative.
4. Although spelling and grammar errors are allowed some latitude within the marking of the assessment, it is advisable to ensure that you use clear, precise, professional language at all times.
5. You are able to cross reference your attendance note to your interview notes, which can help to reduce duplication and save time. However, if you are to use this approach successfully, you will need to ensure that there is a similarity of format between the interview notes and the attendance note. This may also require you to consider using section numbering within the interview.

8.3 Attendance Notes Use and Form

With the process of assessment considered, it would be helpful for us to take a step back to consider the approach that is taken to the production of an attendance note in legal practice.

Attendance notes are vital legal documents as they serve a number of purposes within the legal process.

At the outset, the initial attendance note provides a formal record of the initial meeting with the client, which forms the basis upon which the matter proceeds. For example, it is the attendance note that will likely guide the legal professional as they seek to confirm in writing the instructions that they have been given by the client. This will be documented via a formal letter and will then typically form part of both the client care process and the client's file.

Documenting such initial instructions is essential in ensuring the smooth passage of the case and also provides evidence to the solicitor should a client seek to dispute the standard of service offered at a later stage. The note also helps to ensure that client confidence is established and maintained as the case progresses. For example, any solicitor who has to continually ask the client to repeat instructions is unlikely to be considered positively by the client during the matter at hand.

In addition, the note also serves as an aide memoire to the solicitor. Depending upon the area of law, solicitors can be expected to manage considerable numbers of files simultaneously and it would be unusual for anyone to remember the details of each case with sufficient accuracy. The note then allows the solicitor to quickly refer back and refresh their own recollections of the case and the client.

Of course, legal practices are often highly collaborative in nature, and so it is common for supervisors to seek updates on files, for colleagues to work collectively on a matter, or even for the conduct of the matter to be transferred to a colleague on either a temporary or a permanent basis. The accumulated notes allow others within the firm to become acquainted with the matter at hand, from the initial interview through to the last task completed. It is, therefore, important to ensure that time is devoted each day to update those files that have been worked on during that day.

Perhaps most significantly, the process of updating a file via the addition of contemporaneous attendance notes plays a vital role in both protecting the solicitor from allegations of professional negligence and keeping an up-to-date record of costs.

Notes help a solicitor to challenge allegations of both breaches of conduct and negligent advice through documenting exactly what was said, what was advised, and what was confirmed back to the client as well. Similarly, an effective note helps a legal professional to demonstrate compliance with code of conduct requirements. This is particularly relevant in regards to section 3 – Service and Competence.

As an example, an attendance note which confirms that a client's request for information has been responded to assists in demonstrating compliance with paragraph 3.2, "You ensure that the service you provide to clients is competent and delivered in a timely manner".

The note also typically ends with details of the time spent on the task identified within the note itself. This can be important should a future bill be challenged by a client or should costs be disputed by either the opponent or the court.

8.4 What Requires Recording

As a starting point, it is important to note that there is no universal set format or template in the completion of an attendance note. In practice, it is often the case that each legal practice will have a set style that tends to be passed down from one generation of lawyers to the next as part of the training process. The variety of approaches is also further compounded by the proliferation of different case management software solutions that all provide their own take on the attendance note as part of the move towards digital legal services.

As well as the wide-ranging approach to note format, it is also often the case that individual conventions can also apply to individual legal service providers. This may include everything from approaches where the note is narrative-based with a view to documenting the interaction in fully formed sentences through to the use of in-house notation such as 'Tel' – used to confirm that a telephone call had been made or received on a matter.

Despite the fact that the format of a note is far from universal, we can confirm what is expected by the SQE2 examiner through consideration of the SRA Assessment Specification.

This states that a number of matters must be recorded in the attendance note, including:

- The relevant facts contained within the assessment documentation and that is obtained during the client interview. Relevant facts are the details that are important in ensuring that the client's needs and objectives are met and that are relevant to the completion of correct legal analysis.
- The steps to be taken, post the completion of the interview, that will ensure the case progresses as advised. This would likely include recording that a letter of advice will be sent to the client and a note of any further information or documentation that the client has been requested to provide.
- Advice that is relevant to the client and the matter at hand. This should demonstrate that the candidate has a thorough understanding of the case and the client's concerns and goals. This would likely include demonstrating that the advice addresses the client's matter, consideration of any relevant commercial considerations, and even shows an understanding of the client's personal circumstances.
- The identification of the relevant fundamental legal principles and the correct application of these to the matter at hand. Note that the interviews will be on the subjects of property law, wills, and estate administration.
- Writing an attendance note that is of sufficient detail covering both the context of the client's case and the relevant factual and legal issues. In completing the assessment, the candidates should be aware of relevant ethical and professional conduct issues. These should be addressed in accordance with SRA principles and the Code of Conduct.

With such a prescribed set of requirements to cover, it may be advised to adopt a systematic approach to the design of an attendance note with a view to guiding the process via a template.

A suggested approach would be as follows:

File Reference:
Client Name:
Fee Earner:
Date:
Time:
Header:
Details:
Facts/Concerns:
Advice provided:
Follow up steps:
Time recorded:

Of course, this could be amended or adapted to meet the particular approach that a candidate may be most comfortable with. However, it would be advisable to ensure that the note structure is logical, that it flows from the approach taken to the interview, that it is supported in the approach taken to the recording of interview notes, and that it is clear as to what the candidate needs to consider in each section.

Whilst some of the previous headings are self-explanatory, it is important to consider a few additional considerations.

8.5 Referencing a File

Within legal practice, there is little that concerns a solicitor more than finding a document on their desk which is not associated with a file. This issue only worsens as we work across an increasing number of files in a firm that may have many thousands of ongoing matters.

Sometimes, the issue can be easily resolved as it is rare to find any legal document that does not contain a client's name. However, it is a different case if the document contains a very common name, or perhaps contains just a surname, or is perhaps something that you picked up in error from the photocopier and do not know who it may belong to.

The use of a correct referencing system is, therefore, important to ensure that documents end up in the correct file.

Again, in these days of digitisation, the process of referencing is often taken out of our hands. However, it should be noted that the SQE2 assessment is handwritten, and, as you will note in our example questions in Chapter 7, you will not always be given a reference to use.

It can, therefore, be worthwhile to ensure that you have a clear approach in mind as to how to create a file reference.

For example, a simple suggestion would be to utilise a simple three-part process. For example, if a solicitor called Harvey Massey opened a file for his 350th client and that client was called Uzma Javed, a suitable file reference may be HM/350/UJ – signifying that this is Harvey's file, it is file number 350 and that the client's initials are UJ.

It is clear that this could be approached in a number of ways, and again, you should look to use a system that you are comfortable with.

8.6 Legal Analysis and Advice

As noted previously, the assessment criteria for the attendance note requires that all 'relevant' facts are recorded. It would, therefore, be incorrect to approach the completion of the note as a means to simply write as much as you can in the time available. Instead, candidates are required to focus their attention on the key information provided. This should be documented via a summary rather than in a verbatim format.

With the relevant facts about the client recorded, a systematic approach can then be taken to outline the advice given and the options discussed. The focus should be on demonstrating an understanding of how the law applies to the facts of the case and, therefore, why the selected options have been discussed.

One important area to ensure here is that you tackle any specific queries raised within either the pre-interview documentation or any specific issue discussed within the interview itself. A failure to document a client's concern and a suggested solution to this would likely result in an unsuccessful outcome.

When documenting your response, it is always important to bear in mind that you are not required to be descriptive here – stating what you said is unlikely to provide sufficient detail. Instead, candidates are advised to ensure that their analysis of the legal issue is comprehensive. For example, any review of options available includes adequate consideration of the advantages and disadvantages of selecting a particular option.

8.7 Timing and Billing

It is often the case that the final line of the attendance note could be considered the most important, as it is in your time recording that you are able to record your hours whilst demonstrating both your understanding and your commercial awareness.

Again, it is important to note how the interview and the attendance note process must work together. At the start of the interview, it is important to note the time at which the appointment commenced. It is then vitally important to also end the interview by recording the time of completion.

These two simple but easy to overlook steps ensure that you can complete the attendance note through either adding in the number of minutes that the interview process took to complete or the number of units – if you are more comfortable with unit-based calculations.

8.8 Oversights and Errors

It is a rare solicitor who has not, at some stage in their career, overlooked asking a client for a simple piece of information as part of the initial meeting. This could be a telephone number, a date of birth, a postcode, or an e-mail address. Rest assured, it happens and is often dealt with quickly and easily through either a quick call or perhaps a follow-on meeting.

Whilst these occurrences can be embarrassing, they do not tend to be an impediment to the ongoing conduct of the case. Of course, this may be a different matter if this happens during an interview that forms part of your SQE2 assessment.

Similarly, if a point has been missed due to issues with time management, then this can be problematic.

Should you be in a position where a matter is not addressed, is overlooked, or is recorded incorrectly, then it is important to note that the attendance note can be a real help. By using the attendance note as a means to acknowledge that a mistake has occurred, a candidate can look to gain marks that may mean the difference between a pass or a fail.

A suggested approach would be to highlight with the note the error or omission that has occurred before then stating what future action is needed to remedy the issue.

For example,

> "It was noted that the client was not provided with details regarding all four options available. I will ensure that this is remedied via the letter of advice in which I will highlight option four and the relative advantages and disadvantages of the approach".

In Summary

Plan, manage and progress legal cases and transactions

A competent legal professional will be able to:

- Apply relevant processes and procedures to progress the matter effectively
- Meet deadlines and keep clients informed of progress

Case and transaction management

Trainee solicitors must begin to acquire skills in managing and running a case or transaction.

Trainees must demonstrate the ability to understand the importance of:

- Planning out phases of work to include time, cost, and risk management
- Developing techniques to diarise, follow up, and revisit matters at the appropriate time
- Keeping accurate records and attendance notes
- Effectively managing files
- Regularly and fully reporting back to clients
- Coordinating teams to review progress and revise options

Managing themselves and their own work

Initiate, plan, prioritise, and manage work activities and projects to make sure that they are completed efficiently, on time, and to an appropriate standard, including:

- Clarifying instructions so as to agree on the scope and objectives of the work
- Meeting timescales, resource requirements, and budgets
- Monitoring and keeping other people informed of progress
- Dealing effectively with unforeseen circumstances
- Paying appropriate attention to detail
- Making effective use of information management systems (whether electronic or hard copy), including storing and retrieving information
- Complying with confidentiality, security, data protection, and file retention and destruction requirements

Key Practice Case

Solicitors Regulation Authority v Baljinder Hayre *SDT 11834–2018*

The tribunal heard in SRA v Hayre that the solicitor was admitted in 2002 and was the owner and sole principal of Hayre & Co, which closed after the High Court ruling in 2016.

He was instructed by RK, on behalf of Company X, to buy a plot of land in Bradford for £1.7m. Later, he was instructed to sell part of the land to NK. Bank A was the lender in both instructions. Mr Hayre acted for RK and the company, NK, and the bank in both transactions.

Mr Hayre filed a plan with the Land Registry, which reduced the value of the main plot of land by leaving several access points within the plot now owned by NK.

RK said he was "unable to develop the land as planned".

The SDT found that, despite his denials, Mr Hayre had filed an incorrect plan which encumbered his client's land, breaching the code of conduct by failing to act in the client's best interests or provide an acceptable standard of service.

Mr Hayre was also found to have falsified file attendance notes and relied on those notes in his defence of a civil claim, showing a lack of integrity and dishonestly in doing so – allegations he denied.

He was found to have acted for Company X and NK in the land transactions where there was a conflict of interest, which he admitted.

Deciding to strike him off, the SDT concluded that Mr Hayre's misconduct was motivated by a desire to "avoid a claim by a disgruntled client and to avoid potential disciplinary proceedings".

Practice Tips

- The process of legal analysis requires that you identify at an early stage the evidence that is pertinent to the matter at hand.
- Take the time to evaluate a range of options that may be available to resolve the matter. It may not always be a strictly legal approach that is the best option.
- Ensure that you ensure that clients are aware of their responsibilities in regards to the retention of key evidence.
- Identify the potential risk factors that may impact upon the case proceeding to a successful outcome.
- Ensure that you ensure that the record of the interview is sufficient to allow others to understand the parameters of the case whilst also ensuring that this is succinct to enhance readability.

Practice Risks

- A failure to correctly identify the evidence that is required to support the case can lead to a case that, from the outset, may be doomed to fail, costing time, money, and effort.
- A lack of consideration of all possible options can lead to a case moving in a direction that is sub-optimal. This could lead to issues with the client, the opposing party, and even the court.

- Any failure to advise clients on areas such as document retention can have a significant impact on the client, the case, and your own professional standing.
- Without an adequate understanding of the case, it is easy for the matter to have an unsuccessful outcome, as risk mitigation is not present.
- Failure to adequately communicate the matter can lead to confusion and key areas being missed.

Exercises

EXERCISE A

Research the following methods of note-taking with a view to identifying the strengths and weaknesses of each approach for the completion of a legal note-taking exercise:

- The Alberta Method
- The two-column approach
- The Identification Method
- Cornell Style and the 5R's
- Outline Format
- Mapping

EXERCISE B

Test 1

Which aspects of the SRA code of conduct are likely to be breached if we do not maintain an accurate record of client instructions?

A. Paragraphs 3.1, 3.2, 3.3 and 3.4
B. Paragraphs 3.1, 3.2, 4.1 and 5.1
C. Paragraphs 3.1, 3.2, 6.1 and 6.3
D. Paragraphs 3.2, 3.2, 6.4 and 8.1
E. Paragraphs 1.1, 3.1, 3.2 and 6.1

Test 2

Identify the steps in legal analysis in the correct order.

A. Analyse the law, collect the facts, create logical legal arguments
B. Collect the facts, analyse the law, create logical legal arguments
C. Collect the facts, create logical legal arguments, analyse the law
D. Create logical legal arguments, collect the facts, analyse the law
E. None of the above

Self-Reflection Checklist

What three important things have you learnt from this chapter?	**1**	**2**	**3**
Set out the three additional steps that you need to take to learn the skills in this chapter in more detail.	**1**	**2**	**3**

Suggested Answers

This section provides suggested answers and guidance for approaching exercises and problem questions within this textbook. Some of the answers are intended as a starting point for developing arguments and should not be taken as the definitive list of possible answers for each scenario. The author welcomes any constructive feedback, comments, and suggestions from practitioners, academics, and students on refining the text exercises and case studies for future editions.

Suggested Answers for Chapter 1

Exercise A

The matter represents an issue of potential client conflict, as both of the lenders are seeking to instruct you on the same matter but they will not rank equally due to the parties agreeing that Bowden Bank will take priority.

The relevant section of the code of conduct is CCS 6.2, which states that a law firm must not act for two or more clients in relation to the same matter (or a particular aspect of it) or a related matter (or a particular aspect of it) where the firm's separate duties to act in the best interests of each of those clients would conflict, or there is a significant risk that those duties may conflict. The position is the same for individual solicitors under Rule 6.2 of the SRA Code of Conduct for Solicitors, RELs, and RFLs.

Based upon 6.2, the correct advice would be to decline to act for Brown Financial in this transaction. However, both Bowden Bank and Brown Financial have a clear common purpose in this transaction – namely, they are both seeking to lend money.

It is also noted that the lenders have agreed on their respective rankings and the form of the deed of priority. In addition, the actual legal work required for both parties is similar and the work is related to the same transaction. This would provide the parties with the opportunity to lower costs by having just one set of legal costs.

A further consideration is that the two clients in the scenarios are both financial institutions and would therefore be considered as sophisticated legal clients and so it may therefore be possible to act under 6.2 if:

1. Both clients give written consent.
2. Effective safeguards are established as part of the process to ensure that code of conduct requirements under 6.3, 6.4, and 6.5 are in place regarding confidentiality.
3. The legal practice and the solicitor involved consider it reasonable to act.

Exercise B

Test 1

Answer: B. The receiver's ability to understand the message. The receiver's ability to understand the message depends on their interpretation of the words, tone, body language, and context. Without proper comprehension, the intended meaning of the message may be lost or distorted, and in legal situations, it is essential that precise details are given and understood.

Test 2

Answer: B. Verbal communication uses words, while nonverbal communication uses body language, facial expressions, and tone of voice. Understanding verbal and non-verbal communication is crucial for effective interpersonal relationships, professionally and personally, as it allows us to interpret the intentions and emotions of others better and convey our messages more accurately.

Suggested Answers for Chapter 2

Exercise A

Under SRA Principle 7, Pablo has a duty to act in Lydia's best interests. In doing so, he must consider the requirement in CCS 3.1. He must act only on instructions from Lydia or from someone properly authorised to provide instructions on her behalf.

Pablo must also consider whether Lydia is vulnerable because of her personal circumstances, and his assessment could reveal one of the following:

1. Lydia has the mental capacity to make decisions and give instructions but needs extra support to do this because of mental and/or physical disabilities, which make her vulnerable.
2. Lydia lacks the mental capacity to make decisions and provide instructions, so the statutory and other safeguards must be implemented.
3. Lydia is vulnerable to undue influence and may or may not have the mental capacity to make decisions and provide instructions.

Lydia contacted the firm herself, so at this stage, ostensibly, it is Lydia who is providing instructions. However, in view of her plans for her house, the gift to Jack, and alterations to her will, Pablo should also consider whether Lydia is at risk of undue influence, most obviously in relation to the money she is planning to give to Jack. Pablo needs to be mindful of the pressure that family members can place on each other and should be on his guard that James may have persuaded Lydia to sell her home, give him money, and change her will in his favour. As this is a lifetime gift, a presumption of undue influence may be assumed.

Pablo should arrange to see Lydia on her own so that he can discuss her plans for her property and assess her mental capacity to give instructions for each of the proposed transactions.

In relation to the will, STEP Code 4(iv) also requires that to remove or mitigate the risk of undue influence, a solicitor must "endeavour to ensure that no member of the testator's family, or an intended beneficiary under the will, is present during the meeting".

If Lydia does not agree to see Pablo alone, STEP Code Code 4 (iv) states that if the will drafter feels able to proceed with the interview, they must:

A. Provide a careful explanation of the potential for challenge to the terms of the will; and
B. Take careful note of the third party's participation in the meeting in order to assist with any later dispute.

If Pablo is in any doubt as to Lydia's mental capacity or is unable to form a view, he should arrange a medical opinion about her capacity to make the relevant decisions and to instruct him.

Exercise B

Test your Knowledge – Multiple Choice Tests

Test 1

Answer: C. As employees of an SRA-regulated firm, the legal assistants are subject to the Code of Conduct for Firms.

The Code of Conduct for Firms applies to authorised firms and their managers and employees. Employees is interpreted widely and includes paralegals and legal assistants.

Test 2

Answer: E. Provide the client with technical legal explanations wherever possible.

The solicitor must avoid using technical legal explanations wherever possible and must communicate and explain in a way that is suitable for the client to understand. This is a requirement of CCS 8.6.

Suggested Answers for Chapter 3

Exercise A

Phase 1 illustrates how much we rely on some form of positive feedback when we are speaking to someone. A complete lack of response of any kind (either verbal or non-verbal) can make us feel that we are not being listened to. There is a fine line between no response and passive listening.

Passive listening techniques include:

- Constructive use of silence
- Using non-verbal communication to encourage further disclosure
- Unobtrusive use of verbal responses which do not interrupt or distract the speaker

Exercise B

There is no specific feedback to this question. Ensure that you have critically reflected on your responses to the exercise.

Suggested Answers for Chapter 4

Exercise A

1.	Solicitor:	Please take a seat, Mr Clarke.
2.	Client:	Thank you very much.
3.	Solicitor:	Right now, Mr Clarke, how can I help? (OPEN)
4.	Client:	Er, it's a long story, and I don't really know where to start.
5.	Solicitor:	All right, if I can just go through a few initial questions with you then. I understand a claim has been made against you by Bathright for non-payment of a bill. Is that correct? (CLOSED)
6.	Client:	Yes, that's right.
7.	Solicitor:	It's for £16,000? (CLOSED)
8.	Client:	Yes.
9.	Solicitor:	Why didn't you pay for the bathroom? Were you overcharged? Couldn't you afford to pay? (LEADING and multiple questions difficult to answer)
10.	Client:	No.
11.	Solicitor:	Can you tell me what happened? (OPEN)
12.	Client:	Well, back in April.
13.	Solicitor:	Last year? (CLOSED)
14.	Client:	No, this year. I saw an advert in the local paper saying.
15.	Solicitor:	*The Messenger* or the *Evening News*? (CLOSED)
16.	Client:	In *The Messenger*, saying . . .

The overuse of closed questions is closing down the conversation. The solicitor interrupts the client, and you get the impression that the client is volunteering less and less information as the conversation becomes more restricted. The use of the open question at no.3 should have been followed up with some encouragement from the solicitor to start at the beginning.

Exercise B

Would Mrs Khan prefer a home visit? (This is unlikely to be appropriate, as, at this stage, she does not want her husband to know that she is seeking a divorce).

Is Mrs Khan able to get to the office, and if so, is there a preferred time for an appointment at the office? (Visually impaired clients may find it easier to travel outside peak times when public transport and streets are less busy).

If Mrs Khan is unfamiliar with the office, can a member of staff help guide her to the office from the street or from her transport? (If a client is finding their own way to the office on their own, assistance should be offered to help them find the office).

Does Mrs Khan have a facility to record the meeting so that she can go back over the discussions if she needs to? If not, the firm should offer recording facilities, such as a digital recorder. (As she is severely visually impaired, she will not be able to take written notes).

Make all staff involved in the client interview aware that Mrs Khan is severely visually impaired.

On the day of the appointment, check the reception area, toilets, corridors, and the interview room to make sure they are clear of potential tripping hazards.

After the appointment and when setting up the matter on the case management system, ensure that Mrs Khan's matter is flagged so that anyone dealing with the case is aware of her visual impairment.

Suggested Answers for Chapter 5

Exercise A

For feedback, use an online legal dictionary (for example, the Plain English Campaign A to Z of legal phrases (plainenglish.co.uk) and find the legal term.

Review whether your explanation is clear and understandable.

Exercise B

Legal problem: You may have identified that the client's GP delayed making a referral for symptoms that turned out to be caused by cancer. There could potentially be a claim for clinical negligence.

Feelings: Anger, fear, frustration, sadness, disbelief, vengefulness.

Suggested Answers for Chapter 6

Exercise A

Example 1 demonstrates the most optimal of the three, with some attempt to acknowledge the feelings of the client. It is also clear here that there is some allowance provided for the client to express themselves and to provide the interviewer with some understanding of the impact that the accident has had beyond the injury, the employment, etc.

Example 2 shows some understanding of the emotional impact of the accident, and there is some attempt to demonstrate sympathy and understanding. However, it would be ill-advised to look to downplay the client's feelings through an attempt to explain the behaviour that has been experienced following the accident. As a legal professional, it can be tempting to attempt to explain away everything as if it is a legal issue that can be solved. The response of the work colleagues does not require explanation; it simply requires understanding.

The offer of a drink may be appropriate in allowing a client to collect their thoughts and compose themselves. It can be a positive consideration. However, it is aligned here with a clear indication of the interviewer's partial annoyance at the interview moving beyond the strict pathway that the interviewer intends to follow. It is more a means of escaping responding to the client directly than it is a helpful gesture.

The final example is an even more direct form of failing to address the client's need to discuss impact. It is an excellent example of a failure to engage with the process of active listening. This is likely to result in a client who begins to editorialise her responses, which will likely lead to a case where the solicitor may well miss important information.

Exercise B

As you will have likely noted, the process of the interview is dominated by a series of closed questions that do not allow the client the opportunity to speak freely about the events that resulted in her injury. It should be noted that the use of closed questions may well not have been the intention of the interviewer.

However, the client's hesitation quickly led to the interviewer approaching the interview in this manner.

The failure to allow free conversation results in an interview which is going to be challenging on a number of fronts. Firstly, from the client's perspective, they are likely feeling uncomfortable at the constant firing of questions. There is also the likelihood that the client will be more reserved when answering as she awaits the solicitor asking the specific question that follows. This can greatly inhibit the ability of the client to express a wider range of views to the interviewer in terms of impact, details around the event, and in the building of rapport with the legal advisor.

It should be noted that the approach is less than ideal for the solicitor as well. In addition to the points regarding rapport and the potential for detail to be missed, it is also likely a much more challenging interview for the solicitor as they are required to constantly think about the next question to ask.

The question, answer, question approach also leads to a lack of empathy with the client's situation as there is little consideration of the client's feelings, and there is even a lack of enquiry about the extent of the injury – despite the importance of this is assessing the merits of the case.

It would, therefore, be suggested that the questioning approach could be improved through the use of open question structures, and the interviewer should stick with this approach even in light of the client's initial reluctance (which his actions seem to reinforce).

Suggested Answers for Chapter 7

Exercise A

THE FOLLOWING DOCUMENT SHOULD NOT BE READ BY THE INTERVIEWER PRIOR TO THE INTERVIEW

The Advice (In Outline)

This scenario is based on a mortgage default where the mortgagors (borrower) have failed to keep up with their mortgage repayments. Your advice should be based on the following points:

1. Moneyhive has the power to sell the house to recover the outstanding mortgage debt and costs of selling the house (such as conveyancer, valuation agent, and estate agent fees). This power is normally given in the mortgage contract. It is also provided in the Law of Property Act 1925 (s. 101). However, a lender cannot sell the mortgaged property at once after the default, as there is a statutory requirement of giving a notice in writing. They can only go to court for an 'order for sale' if the borrower fails to resume payment within three months of such notice (s 103).
2. It is possible for the borrower to make an application for a 'time order' to postpone the sale. The lenders want a vacant possession of the mortgaged property so they can attract potential buyers. Therefore, they apply for vacant possession of the mortgaged property at the same time as the 'order for sale'. However, in response to the lender's application for a vacant possession, the borrower can apply to postpone the possession order (Administration of Justice Act 1980, s 36) or apply for a time order (Consumer Credit Act 1974, s 129). In both cases, the borrower will have to satisfy the court that they can resume payment within a reasonable time. This can be satisfied by showing that the borrower has received an offer of employment or they are going to receive an inheritance very soon. The court has more discretionary power to make amendments and variations of the mortgage terms, payments, and interest rates under the CCA 1974 (s. 136) in comparison to the Administration of Justice Act 1980.
3. In the absence of a resumption of payment, the likely outcome is that the property will be sold to recover the mortgage debt. The risk of eviction and the resulting risk of homelessness of minor children of the borrower is one of the

factors that the court can take into account to postpone a possession and/or sale order, but the court is reluctant to make the lender wait for a long time.

4. The borrowers can be sued by the lender for any outstanding mortgage debt within six years of default for outstanding interest payment and 12 years for outstanding debt (capital) (Limitation Act 1980, s 20).
5. The solicitor is bound by the principle of confidentiality, so s/he cannot disclose anything to Mr McGregor's wife unless he consents or the solicitor is required by law to disclose (for instance, where such disclosure would prevent or prosecute a serious crime).
6. This is a professional conduct matter. Solicitors have to abide by a professional code of conduct where they must avoid unprofessional behaviour with clients, which includes engagement outside of professional capacity. This is to ensure that the highest professional standard of the profession is upheld and professional independence is maintained. By knowing personal secrets, a solicitor may not be able to act independently as they might be under an obligation to report certain things to the authorities. Therefore, a solicitor must reject the offer and explain the reason for doing so. The indication by Mr McGregor that that he may not instruct the firm if the offer is not accepted must not have any effect on making an independent and just decision by the solicitor.

Exercise B

THE FOLLOWING DOCUMENT SHOULD NOT BE READ BY THE INTERVIEWER PRIOR TO THE INTERVIEW

The Advice (In Outline)

The scenario requires the interviewer to consider three different issues. The validity of the will, the deceased's intention, and the ability of the law to make reasonable provisions for dependents.

Validity and Intention

In order to make a valid will, Paige must have had the required capacity and must have intended to make a will. Validity requires that s.9 Wills Act 1837 must be complied with.

Within the scenario, it is also clear that the correct formalities for a will have not been followed, as neither witness was present at the same time to witness Paige's signature. This would be a breach of section 9.

A will itself is typically considered to meet part of the requirements for demonstrating intention. However, this initial presumption is rebuttable if it can be evidenced that Paige was induced to write the will by force, fear, fraud, or undue influence.

Within the scenario, Tony observes Eduardo shout at Paige and comments that Paige seemed frightened. If Tony would be willing to provide evidence to this effect, then it may be possible to rebut the presumption.

The validity of the will could also be challenged on the basis of capacity. Again, the scenario confirms that Paige has been suffering from issues of confusion, forgetfulness, and drifting. It is noted that Paige did visit the GP regarding this, and Tony can again evidence the issue of Paige's inability to recognise a neighbour of more than 10 years. So, the client might bring a legal challenge to the validity of the will.

Conclusion

If the will was found to be invalid, the original will would stand.

Reasonable Provision

There is the possibility of a claim being made under the Inheritance (Provision for Families and Dependants) Act 1975. A claim would require evidence that the new will does not make reasonable financial provision for Chris. As noted in the scenario, Chris may be able to bring a claim under section 1(1)(e), namely that "any person who immediately before the death of the deceased was being maintained, either wholly or partly, by the deceased" should have reasonable provision made for them.

This would again require evidence, and it is confirmed that there will be both rent payment records and bank statements that will be able to show a history of payments by Paige.

This would not be conclusive in regards to any claim, as the court is required to consider both Chris's financial position and also that of Eduardo.

It should also be noted that any claim needs to be made within six months from the date of issue of the Grant of Representation.

In Concluding Advice to Chris, it Would be Advised to Consider the Following Options

Do Nothing

Advantages:

- No liability for costs
- The client will not be involved in what could be a long and protracted legal process, which may be time-consuming and stressful

Disadvantages:

- Choosing to take no action will mean that Eduardo will inherit Paige's estate, and Chris may become homeless and destitute.

Commence Court Proceedings to Challenge the Validity of the New Will and/or to Commence a Claim for Reasonable Provision Under the Inheritance (Provision for Families and Dependants) Act 1975

Advantages:

- Should the evidence from neighbours, doctors, and via bank and rental documents confirm the details from the scenario, then it appears that Chris will have a strong case. Should the legal action be successful and the will declared invalid, then Chris would be entitled to the whole of Paige's estate as per the original will.
- The commencement of court proceedings may, in itself, lead to Eduardo offering to resolve the case to all party's mutual satisfaction. Should this occur, then the time, cost, and stress would be reduced.

Disadvantages:

- If the case goes to trial, this will take time and is likely to be very costly and stressful.
- The evidence, although strong, is not conclusive and does rely on others willing to be involved. The burden of proof is on Chris to prove that the will is invalid, and we are unaware of what may be within the medical records or even if neighbours would be happy to provide statements to support the capacity argument.
- Court proceedings involve an element of risk, and Chris cannot know what arguments or documentation Eduardo may have to rebut the claim.

Negotiation

Advantages:

- Should the evidence from neighbours, doctors, and via bank and rental documents confirm the details of the scenario, then it appears that Chris is in a strong bargaining position.
- In addition, Chris has a number of angles that he can use in seeking a negotiated settlement.
- Similarly, Chris appears to have a strong basis for a claim under the I(PFDA)75.
- Whilst neighbours may be reluctant to become involved in formal legal proceedings, they may be more willing to assist if the matter is subject to the more informal option of negotiation.
- Negotiation is likely to be much less costly, less stressful, and time-consuming than bringing court proceedings.
- The court process requires that parties attempt to resolve the matter via negotiated means.

Disadvantages:

- Negotiation requires parties to compromise strict legal positions, and as such, Chris may receive less than he would under a formal legal approach.
- An effective bargaining position still requires Chris to ensure that he has evidence from a range of sources, including neighbours, who may refuse.
- If Eduardo does not engage in the negotiation, it could add to the costs and time involved before starting court proceedings.

Suggested Answers for Chapter 8

Exercise A

The Alberta Method

The Alberta method divides the page into three columns. In the far-left column, the interviewer records general information provided by the client during the appointment. In the middle column, these general themes are given more specificity with greater detail provided, leading into the final column where case-specific information, outcomes, and advice are noted.

Advantages:
The method helps to ensure that there is an organised structure to the note-taking process, with each column helping to move the process from initial law through to legal considerations and then onto case-specific details.

Disadvantages:
The process of using the approach takes practice and can lead to confusion as to where information goes – is it column 1 or column 2. It is also a very narrative approach, lacking the visual benefits of other systems. It can also require additional time to prepare notes pages.

The two-column approach

The two-column method is a variation of the Alberta method and the Cornell method. The method uses two columns, with the first being the take notes column – where notes from the interview are recorded to provide a record of the discussion. The second column is the make notes column, where the interviewer records prompts, observations, advice, and next steps information. It can be viewed that the left column is what the client says, whilst the second column is more what the interviewer thinks.

Advantages:
The method helps to ensure that there is an organised structure to the note-taking process without the complication of adding numbers of columns and sections that

can easily confuse the process. The approach can be highly intuitive and can be a useful starting point for a person new to recording interview discussions.

Disadvantages:

The process can oversimplify the note-taking process and can lead to large amounts of information remaining unstructured, which can hamper review. The non-graphical nature of the note-taking method also increases the time required to decipher the content. The process can be confusing for others to follow should they need to review the notes themselves.

The Cornell Method

The Cornell method is a structured note-taking system that allows you to organise your notes to facilitate review and self-assessment. The process involves dividing the note page into three sections: on the left is a cues/questions column, on the right is the main notes space, and at the bottom of each page is a summary section.

The cue/questions column is used as a space where cues and questions are written that can prompt the interviewer to address topics or to return to particular themes. The main notes space is used to provide a narrative set of notes based upon the client's responses and information provided. Finally, the summary space is provided to record next steps, initial advice, and outcomes.

Advantages:

The method helps to ensure that there is an organised structure to the note-taking process, and the cue column can be essential in ensuring that a point that requires further exploration can be returned to without interrupting the client in full flow. The summary section is also a useful way of structuring the end of the conversation and as an aid to memory.

Disadvantages:

The process of using the approach takes considerable practice and needs a good level of legal knowledge on which to base the cues. It is also a very narrative approach, lacking the visual benefits of other systems. It can also be problematic to ensure concise notes are available as the page is filled with the structure, restricting free flow.

Outline Format

Dash or indented outlining is an approach where the most general information begins at the left of the page, with details becoming more specific as we move across to the right-hand side. In the system, the relationships between the different pieces of information are carried out through indenting with no requirement for the note-taker to use numbers, letters, or Roman numerals.

The method involves listening to the interviewee and then writing points in an organised pattern based on clear indentation of content across the page. Major points are placed farthest to the left, with each more specific point, then indented in various degrees as we move towards the right. The system highlights the level of importance of a particular note based upon the distance from each of the major points recorded.

Advantages:
A well-organised system that both records information and relates each point with increased specificity. The system is effective in reducing editing and can enhance the process of review by graphically displaying information.

Disadvantages:
The process can be complicated to apply consistently in complex matters. The system can also be disrupted by errors in placing information, and this can occur when a lot of information is provided or is provided rapidly.

Mapping

The mapping method uses a graphic system of interconnected shapes, colours, or themes as a means to relate facts, information, or legal considerations to every other fact or piece of information provided.

Advantages:
This mapping method allows the note-taker to track the information provided during an interview visually. It is an intuitive process that can be highly effective in tracking the story of a case, and it simplifies the process of recall and information sharing through the use of shapes, colours, and numbers.

Disadvantages:
The system can confuse as well as clarify and can lead to a lack of narrative to the interview record.

Exercise B

Test 1

Answer: A. A failure to maintain an accurate record of client instructions is likely to lead to a breach of

3.1 You only act for clients on instructions from the client or from someone properly authorised to provide instructions on their behalf. If you have reason to suspect that the instructions do not represent your client's wishes, you do not act unless you have satisfied yourself that they do. However, in circumstances where you have legal authority to act, notwithstanding that it is not possible to obtain or ascertain the instructions of your client, then you are subject to the overriding obligation to protect your client's best interests.
3.2 You ensure that the service you provide to clients is competent and delivered in a timely manner.
3.3 You maintain your competence to carry out your role and keep your professional knowledge and skills up to date.
3.4 You consider and take account of your client's attributes, needs, and circumstances.

Test 2

Answer: B.

The correct order of steps in legal analysis is to collect the facts first, then analyse the law, and finally create logical legal arguments based upon the facts ascertained and the law that underpins the enquiry. This order allows for a systematic approach to understanding the case at hand. By collecting the facts first, one can gather all the relevant information needed to make informed legal arguments. Then, analysing the law helps to determine the applicable legal principles and precedents. Finally, creating logical legal arguments involves using the collected facts and analysed law to construct a persuasive case. It should be noted that the process could be considered as cyclical as the creation of logical legal arguments may require us to revert to the client for additional information constantly.

Index

Note: Page numbers in **bold** indicate a table on the corresponding page.

For Product Safety Concerns and Information please contact our EU representative GPSR@taylorandfrancis.com Taylor & Francis Verlag GmbH, Kaufingerstraße 24, 80331 München, Germany